# Interdisciplinary Curriculum:

# DESIGN
# AND
# IMPLEMENTATION

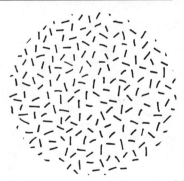

Edited by Heidi Hayes Jacobs

**Association for Supervision
and Curriculum Development**

Copyright 1989 by the Association for Supervision and Curriculum Development, 1250 N. Pitt Street, Alexandria, VA 22314. All rights reserved. ASCD publications present a variety of viewpoints. The views expressed or implied in this publication are not necessarily official positions of the Association.

Printed in the United States of America.

Typeset by Mid-Atlantic Photo Composition, Inc.

Printed by Edwards Brothers, Inc.

Ronald S. Brandt, *Executive Editor*
Nancy Modrak, *Managing Editor, Books*
René M. Townsley, *Associate Editor*
Al Way, *Manager, Design Services*

ASCD Stock No. 611-89156

$13.95

*Library of Congress Cataloging-in-Publication Data*
Interdisciplinary curriculum: design and implementation/edited by
    Heidi Jacobs.
        p.   cm.
      ISBN 0-87120-165-8
      1. Curriculum planning. 2. Interdisciplinary approach in
education. I. Jacobs, Heidi. II. Association for Supervision and
Curriculum Development.
LB2806.15.I57 1989
375'.001—dc20                                                89-38019
                                                                 CIP

# Interdisciplinary Curriculum: Design and Implementation

# Foreword

. *Interdisciplinary Curriculum: Design and Implementation* demystifies curriculum integration. The authors describe a variety of curriculum integration options ranging from concurrent teaching of related subjects to fusion of curriculum focus to residential study focusing on daily living; from two-week units to year-long courses. They offer suggestions for choosing proper criteria for successful curriculum integration, dealing with the attitudes of key individuals and groups, and establishing validity. And they present a step-by-step approach to integration, proceeding from selection of an organizing center to a scope and sequence of guiding questions to a matrix of activities for developing integrated units of study. In addition, the authors make a useful distinction between curriculum—content—and metacurriculum—those learning skills helpful in acquiring the curriculum content being taught and in developing the capacity to think and learn independently.

The book acknowledges that curriculum integration is not a panacea; many integration decisions entail tradeoffs. It also illuminates the value of higher-order thinking and learning skills and provides a vehicle for their integration into curriculum. Indeed, by their practical approach, the authors provide a valuable resource to help teachers avoid the pitfalls of earlier integration efforts.

*Interdisciplinary Curriculum: Design and Implementation* makes a significant contribution to accomplishing ASCD's mission of developing leadership for quality in education for all students.

PATRICIA C. CONRAN
*President, 1989-90*

# 1

# The Growing Need for Interdisciplinary Curriculum Content

**Heidi Hayes Jacobs**

MIKE, A 2ND GRADER, DEFINES MATHEMATICS AS "SOMETHING YOU DO IN THE morning." Unfortunately, his statement reflects an internalization of mathematics as an experience to be absorbed from 9:45-10:30 a.m., and certainly before recess. We rarely explain to students why the school day is designed as it is. It should be no surprise then that students look at the arbitrary divisions for reading, math, social studies, science, art, music, and physical education and begin to define the subject areas as separate bodies of knowledge with little relationship to one another.

As Mike moves into junior and senior high, the subject matter delineations will become even more entrenched as the academic areas are forced into 50-minute time blocks taught by individual specialists. It is no wonder that many secondary school students complain that school is irrelevant to the larger world. In the real world, we do not wake up in the morning and do social studies for 50 minutes. The adolescent begins to realize that in real life we encounter problems and situations, gather data from all of our resources, and generate solutions. The fragmented school day does not reflect this reality.

The British philosopher Lionel Elvin (1977) uses an analogy to describe the problem of the false time constraints of the school day:

> When you are out walking, nature does not confront you for three quarters of an hour only with flowers and in the next only with animals (p. 29).

If we take Elvin's analogy from another angle, it is clear that when out walking, you can also sit and pick up the flowers and concentrate solely on them for three-quarters of an hour and learn a great deal. The problem is that in school we generally do not consider both perspectives as necessary components of a child's education.

Having examined various models and approaches to interdisciplinary design for the past 15 years, I have made some observations. Although teachers have good intentions when they plan interdisciplinary courses, these courses frequently lack staying power. Two problems in content selection often plague courses:

1. *The Potpourri Problem.* Many units become a sampling of knowledge from each discipline. If the subject is Ancient Egypt, there will be a bit of history about Ancient Egypt, a bit of literature, a bit of the arts, and so forth. Hirsch (1987) and Bloom (1987) have criticized this approach for its lack of focus. Unlike the disciplines that have an inherent scope and sequence used by curriculum planners, there is no general structure in interdisciplinary work. Curriculum developers themselves must design a content scope and sequence for any interdisciplinary unit or course.

2. *The Polarity Problem.* Traditionally, interdisciplinarity and the discipline fields have been seen as an either/or polarity, which has promoted a range of conflicts. Not only does the curriculum design suffer from a lack of clarity, but real tensions can emerge among teachers. Some feel highly territorial about their subjects and are threatened as new views of their subject are promoted. There is a need for both interdisciplinary and discipline-field perspectives in design.

To avoid these two problems, effective interdisciplinary programs must meet two criteria.

• They must have carefully conceived design features: a scope and sequence, a cognitive taxonomy to encourage thinking skills, behavioral indicators of attitudinal change, and a solid evaluation scheme.

• They must use both discipline-field-based and interdisciplinary experiences for students in the curriculum. Chapter 2, on design options, spells out the range of these possibilities.

To simply list a set of considerations for selecting interdisciplinary content would be to avoid wrestling with the complexities and possibilities for interdisciplinary work. When Mr. Davis, social studies teacher, and Mrs. Valasquez, English teacher, are sitting in the faculty lounge and decide to do a unit together, there is a chance that their work will fall prey to both the potpourri and the polarity problems. It is essential that they take time to reflect on some fundamental questions. These questions are spelled out in the rest of this chapter in order (1) to establish the need for interdisciplinary possibilities, (2) to define terms used in the field, and (3) to present a set of assumptions to guide effective practice.

## Why Look at Curriculum Integration?

Over the past few years, the interest in and need for curriculum integration has intensified throughout the country for several reasons.[1]

### The Growth of Knowledge

Knowledge is growing at exponential proportions in all areas of study. If you look at one field, such as science, you see the remarkable degree of specialization that has resulted from research and practice. Each area of the curriculum has the blessing and burden of growth. The curriculum planner must wrestle not only with what should be taught but what can be eliminated from the curriculum. In English, there are new writers, new books, and new interpretations to consider every year. In the social sciences, there are difficult questions of selecting focal cultures, for we obviously cannot study every country in the world.

Then there are the annual state education mandates that get passed down to schools based on current problems. For example, many states now require a curriculum covering AIDS. Drug prevention curriculums have been on the books for a number of years in many states. Sex education and family life curriculums now are an

---

[1] A poll conducted by ASCD in 1988 suggested that it is the number one issue among the members of the ASCD National Polling Panel (a sample of organization members, invited guests, Chief State School Officers, and deans of schools of education).

integral part of the public school domain in some areas of the country. These are critical topics, but they do add pressure to the school schedule. The length of the school day in the United States has stayed basically about the same since the 1890s. We need to rethink the ways we select the various areas of study. Knowledge will not stop growing, and the schools are bursting at the seams.

### Fragmented Schedules

I have heard teachers complain hundreds of times, "The day is so fragmented!" Elementary teachers say, "I never see my kids for a prolonged period of time," and secondary school teachers add, "I must plan my lessons to fit 40-minute time blocks rather than the needs of my students."

Schools respond to state requirements by dividing time into blocks to parcel out specific responsibilities and to maintain accountability. Frequently, state requirements are stated in terms of minutes per week. Students feel this fragmentation keenly. One of my favorite means of beginning an assessment of a secondary school is to follow one student through the day. It is easy to forget how, 8 times a day, students leap out of their seats every 40 minutes and rush for 5 minutes to another setting, another subject, another teacher, another set of students.

### Relevance of Curriculum

If we are trying to devise a means of driving students out of school, we obviously are succeeding. Recent estimates suggest that, nationally, 25 percent of students drop out every year and in urban areas as many as 40 percent. Something is very wrong. A common concern of students is the irrelevance of their course work in their lives out of school. They find it difficult to understand why they need math when most of their instruction is based on a textbook used in isolation from its applications. The fragmentation of the day only compounds the dilemma as students never have the chance to explore a subject in depth.

The relevancy issue also strikes a deeper chord. Only in school do we have 43 minutes of math and 43 minutes of English and 43 minutes of science. Outside of school, we deal with problems and concerns in a flow of time that is not divided into knowledge fields.

We get up in the morning and confront the whole of our lives. It is here that relevancy comes into play. It is not that schools should avoid dealing with specific disciplines; rather, they also need to create learning experiences that periodically demonstrate the relationship of the disciplines, thus heightening their relevancy. There is a need to actively show students how different subject areas influence their lives, and it is critical that students see the strength of each discipline perspective in a connected way.

Out of this concern for relevance arises another key area that has been the subject of debate for the past few years: the ignorance of the American public and the lack of cultural literacy (Hirst 1987, Bloom 1987). Some argue that there should be a body of knowledge that is passed on from one generation to the next that deals with our classics and with the basics of our culture: its history and its arts and sciences. The danger in this line of reasoning is to fall prey to the polarity problem. Discounting interdisciplinary efforts as attempts at relevancy at the expense of the classics is simplistic and only heightens the polarity.

The attempts at interdisciplinary work that seem to be most successful are those that address the polarity question in a different way. The question here isn't whether we should teach the classics (though that is a question worthy of genuine discussion); rather, we are considering a larger point: No matter what the content, we can design active linkages between fields of knowledge. We can teach the works of Shakespeare with an eye to the history of the times, the arts, the values, the role of science, and the zeitgeist rather than simply sticking with specific passages. The student who does not possess a literary bent may encounter *King Lear* in another subject area. Integrated curriculum attempts should not be seen as an interesting diversion but as a more effective means of presenting the curriculum, whether you wish to teach Plato or feminist literature. The curriculum becomes more relevant when there are connections between subjects rather than strict isolation.

Consider the definition of "history" given by Ravitch and Finn (1985). They rightly ask us to provide a solid and thorough understanding of history and at the same time to embrace an interdisciplinary perspective beyond

> . . . the memorization of dates and facts or the identification of wars and political leaders, though these have their place. . . .

> Properly conceived, history includes the history of ideas, cultural developments, and social, political, and economic movements. It includes the evolution of diverse cultures and the changing relationships among peoples, races, religions, and beliefs (p. 206).

They recommend a consistent chronological structure to history instruction, which is obviously the sensible route. But, more importantly, their definition of history is encompassing rather than limiting and I believe would enlarge the relevancy of history for the high school student. Ravitch (1985) warns us to beware unwise practices under the banner of relevancy. She is quite right. The definition that she has shaped with Chester Finn serves as a worthy prototype for a dynamic view of history that is, in fact, interdisciplinary.

### Society's Response to Fragmentation

We are coming to recognize that we cannot train people in specializations and expect them to cope with the multifaceted nature of their work. It is not surprising that many of our nation's medical schools now have philosophers-in-residence. A doctor cannot be trained only in physiology and the biology of the body; a doctor treats the whole human being. The ethical questions that confront doctors have a great deal to do with the effectiveness of their treatments on patients. Business schools are providing ethics courses, education schools are providing business administration courses, and so forth. Basically, we have become a specialized world, but the pendulum is swinging toward some balance, so that we may draw from the range of fields to better serve our specific fields. The renewed trend in the schools toward interdisciplinarity will help students better integrate strategies from their studies into the larger world.

# Definitions that Clarify Practice

Many interpretations of the curriculum terminology are used in discussing the integration of knowledge. Sometimes I have heard teachers refer to their "interdisciplinary unit" when, in fact, their meaning of interdisciplinary unit is 180 degrees different from their colleagues' down the hall. It is essential that there be some fundamental agreement for the meanings of the words that will be used to describe the plan that emerges from the design efforts or there can be real confusion. The following are some terms whose definitions attempt to illustrate the shades of difference between conceptions of knowledge. (In Chapter 2 I attempt to provide some practical applications for a number of these terms.)

DISCIPLINE FIELD: A specific body of teachable knowledge with its own background of education, training, procedures, methods, and content areas (Piaget 1972).

The starting point for all discussions about the nature of knowledge in our schools should be a thorough understanding of the disciplines. As Lawton (1975) suggests, each discipline asks different questions. There are distinct frames of reference and kinds of statements, and each of these suggests unique procedures and end results that are in fact the discipline fields. The British thinker Hirst (1964) has studied how best to present knowledge systems to young people. In his view, each discipline is a form of knowledge with separate and distinct characteristics. Within each form are unique concepts and propositions that have tests to validate their truth.

The motivation for discipline divisions is in part based on the notion that the disciplines encourage efficient learning. The structure of the disciplines is necessary for knowledge acquisition. It is fundamental in order to learn how things are related (Bruner 1975). The advantage of the disciplines is that they permit schools to investigate with systematic attention to the progressive mastery of closely related concepts and patterns of reasoning (Hirst and Peters 1974). The decision by educators to specialize goes back to Aristotle, who believed that knowledge should be divided into three arenas: the productive disciplines, the theoretical disciplines, and the practical disciplines.

Certainly the emphasis on discipline-field curriculum in the American public school rests largely on a rationale that cites its instructional effectiveness, inherent conceptual cohesion, and socially sanctioned community base. Yet we rarely discuss with children the reason for dividing the day into discipline areas of focus. As Mike, the 2nd grader in the beginning of this chapter, said, math becomes something we do in the morning. I have spoken with young children who explain, "My teacher likes reading time, you can tell," or "Science is when we use the learning centers." The way the day is divided has more to do with a change in teacher attitude or the use of a part of the room than with any understanding of what a scientist does or the purpose of reading literature. We simply skip telling children why we have planned their school lives in blocks of time. Before any meaningful inter-disciplinary experience can occur, students need to begin to understand the nature of knowledge on a level that is clearly appropriate to their age and experience.

INTERDISCIPLINARY: A knowledge view and curriculum approach that consciously applies methodology and language from more than one discipline to examine a central theme, issue, problem, topic, or experience.

In contrast to a discipline-field based view of knowledge, interdisciplinarity does not stress delineations but linkages. Meeth (1978) notes that the emphasis is on deliberately identifying the relationship between disciplines. It is a holistic approach with a tradition in Western thought that comes from Plato's ideal of unity as the highest good in all things. Interdisciplinarity nurtures a different perspective with focus on themes and problems of life experience.

When examining the relationship between fields of knowledge, there is a range of prefixes that connote various nuances. Consider the following:

CROSSDISCIPLINARY: Viewing one discipline from the perspective of another; for example, the physics of music and the history of math (Meeth 1978).

MULTIDISCIPLINARY: The juxtaposition of several disciplines focused on one problem with no direct attempt to integrate (Piaget 1972, Meeth 1978).

PLURIDISCIPLINARY: The juxtaposition of disciplines assumed to be more or less related; e.g., math and physics, French and Latin (Piaget 1972).

TRANSDISCIPLINARY: Beyond the scope of the disciplines; that is, to start with a problem and bring to bear knowledge from the disciplines (Meeth 1978).

With the exception of the definition for interdisciplinary, experience in the field has made me reticent to use these definitions. They represent important differences in the way the curriculum designer will shape the ultimate unit or course of study, but they are cumbersome, if not esoteric, in conversation. I find that teachers and administrators prefer the more nuts-and-bolts set of terms that is presented in the next chapter. Nevertheless, it seems essential that decisions regarding the curriculum be made with a deliberate consensus as to the kind of discipline-field emphasis that will occur; otherwise, there is the tendency toward the potpourri and a confused melee of activities when a team starts producing the lesson plans. The goal here is to have informed practitioners.

## Support for an Interdisciplinary Curriculum

What are some guiding beliefs and assumptions that will support an interdisciplinary curriculum attempt? The philosophy of the curriculum developer will always permeate the final design. I compare our work to architects who design a project based on a site, materials, and the population to be served. Sometimes in the course of carrying out the project there are unexpected events—a delay in materials, an immovable rock in the foundation—so the architect adapts the plan. But, initially, the architect brings a personal vision to the task. The more aware we are of our philosophical beliefs, the more likely we are to make responsible design choices that reflect a cohesive and lasting quality in the educational experience we are attempting to build. Consider the following beliefs and assumptions as you create your statement of philosophy for interdisciplinary work.

- Students should have a range of curriculum experiences that reflects both a discipline-field and an interdisciplinary orientation. I have hammered away on this point because of my concern that devotees of either position will claim "mine is the only way." Just as pioneering artists like Joyce and Picasso could not break the rules until they had fully mastered them, students cannot fully benefit from interdisciplinary studies until they acquire a solid grounding in the various disciplines that interdisciplinarity attempts to bridge (Jacobs and Borland 1986).
- To avoid the potpourri problem, teachers should be active curriculum designers and determine the nature and degree of integration and the scope and sequence of study. The teacher's decisions will

most directly affect students in the day-to-day running of the classroom. The teacher should be empowered to work as a designer, to shape and to edit the curriculum according to the students' needs.

● Curriculum making is a creative solution to a problem, hence, interdisciplinary curriculum should only be used when the problem reflects the need to overcome fragmentation, relevance, and the growth of knowledge.

● Curriculum making should not be viewed as a covert activity. The interdisciplinary unit or course should be presented to all members of the school community. Few parents will have experienced integrated curriculum, and they will feel less suspicious if they are well informed.

● Students should study epistemological issues. Regardless of the age of students, epistemological questions such as "What is knowledge?", "What do we know?", and "How can we present knowledge in the schools?" can and should be at the heart of our efforts (Jacobs and Borland 1986). The preschool child deserves to know why the room is organized the way it is, why there are "choice times," and why there are set times for "group meetings." Relevance begins with the rationale for educational choices affecting the school life of the student.

● Interdisciplinary curriculum experiences provide an opportunity for a more relevant, less fragmented, and stimulating experience for students. When properly designed and when criteria for excellence are met (Chapter 4, Ackerman), then students break with the traditional view of knowledge and begin to actively foster a range of perspectives that will serve them in the larger world.

● Students can and, when possible, should be involved in the development of interdisciplinary units. The four-step process described in Chapter 5 allows for student input in a meaningful way. It is not always desirable for students to participate, but student interest in the units is often enhanced by their involvement in the planning process (Jacobs and Borland 1986).

By understanding the growing need for curriculum integration programs, clarifying the terminology that will be used in choices made by the curriculum maker, and articulating a set of guiding assumptions, solid and lasting designs will emerge. The hope is that you and your team will become reflective practitioners as you begin your project.

## References

Bloom, A. (1987). *The Closing of the American Mind.* New York: Simon and Schuster.

Bruner, J. (1975). *Toward a Theory of Instruction.* Cambridge: Belknap Press.

Elvin, L. (1977). *The Place of Common Sense in Educational Thought.* London: Unwin Educational Books.

Hirst, P.H., and R.S. Peters. (1074). "The Curriculum." In *Conflicting Conceptions of Curriculum,* edited by E. Eisner and E. Vallance. Berkeley, Calif.: McCutchen.

Hirst, P.H. (1964). *Knowledge and Curriculum.* London: Routledge and Kegan Paul.

Hirsch, E.D., Jr. (1987). *Cultural Literacy.* Boston: Houghton-Mifflin.

Jacobs, H.H., and J.H. Borland. (Winter 1986). "The Interdisciplinary Concept Model. Design and Implementation." *Gifted Child Quarterly.*

Lawton, D. (1975). *Class, Culture, and Curriculum.* Boston: Routledge and Kegan Paul.

Meeth, L.R. (1978). "Interdisciplinary Studies: Integration of Knowledge and Experience." *Change* 10: 6-9.

Piaget, J. (1972). *The Epistemology of Interdisciplinary Relationships.* Paris: Organization for Economic Cooperation and Development.

Ravitch, D. (1985). "Why Educators Resist a Basic Required Curriculum?" In *The Great School Debate,* edited by B. Gross and R. Gross. New York: Simon and Schuster.

Ravitch, D., and C. Finn. (1985). "The Humanities: A Truly Challenging Course of Study." In *The Great School Debate,* edited by B. Gross and R. Gross. New York: Simon and Schuster.

# 2

# Design Options for an Integrated Curriculum

## Heidi Hayes Jacobs

*There is no science but pure science.*
*—Mrs. Jones, Honors Science Teacher*

*How dare we divide the child's day into little parcels*
*of knowledge. There is a whole child there!*
*—Mr. Philips, 4th Grade Teacher*

THERE IS AN UNFORTUNATE TENDENCY FOR SCHOOL ADMINISTRATORS AND teachers to believe that the choice for content design boils down to an either/or proposition between discipline field specialization and interdisciplinary integration. The "polarity issue," as I call it, can and must be avoided in order to foster a long-term curriculum design that will bring power to your program. In this chapter we look at a continuum of design options (Figure 2.1) that explains the range of choices for planning your program.

We consider each option in terms of its characteristics, advantages, and disadvantages, and examples of existing applications of the continuum. Educators have used this continuum as a planning tool to clarify their choices and combine options.

**Figure 2.1**
**Continuum of Options for Content Design**

| Discipline Based | Parallel Disciplines | Multi- Disciplinary | Inter- disciplinary Units/Courses | Integrated Day | Complete Program |
|---|---|---|---|---|---|

# Design Options

### Discipline-Based Content Design

*Characteristics*: The discipline-based content design option focuses on a strict interpretation of the disciplines with separate subjects in separate time blocks during the school day. No attempt for integration is made, in fact, it is avoided. Traditional approaches to subjects such as language arts, mathematics, science, social studies, music, art, and physical education are the usual fare. In secondary programs, these general academic and arts areas break down into more specific fields, such as algebra under mathematics or American history under social studies. There are some variations of block scheduling and the way the week or cycle is programmed. Nevertheless, knowledge is presented in separate fields without a deliberate attempt to show the relationships among them.

*Advantages*: Without question, the discipline-specific option is the most common format used in the United States, and both students and teachers are used to it. Parents usually are familiar with only the discipline field approach. It is efficient because courses of study and statewide goals and objectives are available in each field through all grades, and curriculums, tests, and supplementary materials exist for each field. Focusing on each discipline provides students with specialized skills and concepts in a field. Secondary teachers are generally trained in a special area, thus reinforcing the economic support in the educational establishment for trained specialists. The specialized training gives teachers greater depth of knowledge as they read about current trends in their field and work in professional organizations that provide a sharp focus on best curriculum practices.

*Disadvantages*: The problem with the approach is its fragmenting effect on the student's school day. Students must move from one subject to another, and on the secondary level this usually means movement from one space to another. Teachers are forced to plan activities according to allotted time rather than according to students' needs in relation to the content. On an epistemological level, the primary disadvantage to this form of content construction is that it does not reflect the reality of life outside school. We simply do not function in a world where problems are discipline specific in regimented time blocks. Students do not learn how the perspective of one discipline relates to another.

## Parallel Discipline Designs

*Characteristics*: When the curriculum is designed in a parallel fashion, teachers sequence their lessons to correspond to lessons in the same area in other disciplines. For example, if the social studies teacher teaches a World War II unit in the beginning of spring semester, then the English teacher will reschedule her autumn book, *Summer of My German Soldier*, to coincide with the social studies unit. The content itself does not change, only the order in which it appears. The goal is a simultaneous effect as students relate the studies in one subject with the others. Teachers working in a parallel fashion are not deliberately connecting curriculum across fields of knowledge; they are simply resequencing their existing curriculum in the hope that students will find the implicit linkages.

*Advantages*: This is a relatively painless procedure. Teachers are not changing the design of the curriculum except for one variable: the time of year in which it is taught. Obviously, certain subjects are more flexible than others, and a chronological course such as U.S. history cannot be resequenced. However, the English teacher may be more flexible in sequencing literature choices. The elementary teacher can schedule science lessons on geology in the Southwest to dovetail with a music lesson on *Brighty of the Grand Canyon*. In short, there is concurrent teaching of related subjects.

*Disadvantages*: There are missed opportunities for deliberate, in-depth integration. Since team teaching is avoided, students do not see the way two teaching professionals can add to the dynamics of classroom life. To a degree, students are still studying concepts in isolation and must uncover for themselves the relationships among fields of knowledge.

## Complementary Discipline Units or Courses

*Characteristics:* The complementary option suggests that certain related disciplines be brought together in a formal unit or course to investigate a theme or issue. It is different from parallel teaching, where the focus stays on the prescribed scope and sequence of each discipline. A good analogy is a color wheel and the notion of complementary colors. Just as groups of colors complement one another, certain disciplines are directly related to one another, such as the humanities. Of course, it is possible to design a course that brings together two disciplines of seemingly different characters—as long as the questions shed light on and complement one another (as in a course on "Ethics in Science").

*Advantages:* Lesson planning for bringing several disciplines together requires less effort than a fully interdisciplinary unit. On the secondary level, there are fewer people to bring together. Given that there are obvious links between allied fields of knowledge, the design process can be handled directly. When working in teaming situations, teachers often are more comfortable working in related disciplines. Curriculum materials are generally easier to pull together. In fact, some publishers have started packaging complementary humanities courses. Parent groups seem to have a fairly easy time understanding the validity of a course or unit that brings a few disciplines together.

*Disadvantages:* Any curriculum design that brings change in institutional schedules, planning for a revised content, and money for staff training can prompt resistance. Students will need to reconsider their traditional view of knowledge. As one high school sophomore said, "I used to know how to get an easy A in science, but in this course on Ethical Issues in Science, I can't use my old ways." If you're willing to wrestle with this kind of resistance from students, the challenge can be rewarding. But if the resistance is difficult, you may find the changes demanding.

## Interdisciplinary Units/Courses

*Characteristics:* In this design, periodic units or courses of study deliberately bring together the full range of disciplines in the school's curriculum: language arts, math, social studies, and science; and the arts, music, and physical education. The main point is that the designers attempt to use a full array of discipline-based perspectives.

The units are of specific duration: a few days, a few weeks, or a semester. This option does not purport to replace the discipline-field approach; rather, they are mutually supportive.

*Advantages*: This design fosters a comprehensive epistemological experience. It is stimulating and motivating for students and teachers. Generally, it is easier to set up interdisciplinary units and courses than a complete school program. There is an advantage as teachers can plan their interdisciplinary work around themes and issues that emerge from their ongoing curriculum. Scheduling can be adapted to the school setting; that is, units can last four weeks or eight weeks, depending on the teachers' needs. In short, units can be flexibly designed to fit time constraints.

*Disadvantages*: This model requires effort and change. Generally, interdisciplinary efforts are flawed by the "potpourri" approach, but there are deliberate steps that can enable designers to create a meaningful and carefully orchestrated program. This entails timing, time for planning, and energy on the part of the planners. Funds are needed to support best practices and long-range planning. Parents may have difficulty accepting the value of an interdisciplinary program, because few have experienced the approach in their own schooling. More time is needed to educate the community about this option.

### Integrated-Day Model

*Characteristics*: This model is a full-day program based primarily on themes and problems emerging from the child's world. The emphasis is on an organic approach to classroom life that focuses the curriculum on the child's questions and interests rather than on content determined by a school or state syllabus. The approach originated in the British Infant School movement in the '60s and is most commonly seen in the United States in preschools and kindergarten programs.

*Advantages*: The integrated day is a natural day. Time is structured according to the needs of the students, and the needs of the curriculum are planned around them, rather than institutional demands. Motivation is often high with this approach because the areas of study are directly linked to children's lives.

*Disadvantages*: This model represents a philosophy that is not held by many teachers, and they must believe for it to work effectively.

The approach entails enormous work and planning by teachers because it is not based on an existing curriculum. The management of classroom organization is highly sophisticated and requires specific training. There are no assurances that basic core curriculum requirements will be met, especially with older children.

### Complete Program

*Characteristics*: This approach is the most extreme form of interdisciplinary work. Students live in the school environment and create the curriculum out of their day-to-day lives. Perhaps A.S. Neil's Summerhill is the most widely known example of such an approach. Students who are interested in the buildings on campus might study architecture. If there were a conflict between students concerning ways to behave in the school, they could study rules or government. This is a totally integrated program because the student's life is synonymous with school.

*Advantages*: This is the most integrated program. The life of the student is the focus for the school. Students in much of the Summerhill literature reported feeling empowered by a sense of independence and self-direction. This contrasts to the dependency fostered in more traditional approaches.

*Disadvantages*: This is obviously a radical approach to integration and requires the full commitment of families and school personnel. Given that it is residential, chances are that adolescents rather than young children would be involved. There can be little doubt that the traditional approach to content would not receive attention here. There are no guarantees that students receive exposure to the standard school curriculum.

## Factors to Consider When Selecting an Option

The continuum of options provides a framework for administrators to pick and choose the design configurations that best suit their situations. When determining the combination of interdisciplinary options that you might select, consider the following conditions:

1. The flexibility of your schedule. Are you able to make adjustments in your schedule that will allow you to encourage teaming arrangements or rearrange the sequence of subjects? Time is the basic

currency in education; your ability to create choices rests largely on this fundamental factor. You will be able to develop your curriculum more readily if you have flexibility.

2. The support of your staff. Are your teachers enthusiastic about the possibilities for integration? Without motivation, school change is difficult. Certainly teachers need to see the reasons for restructuring. The greater the degree of integration, the greater the need for preparatory work with your faculty.

Staff members may be more inclined toward gradual change, and it may be wise to begin the change process incrementally. When there is some reluctance to begin with a full-scale interdisciplinary course, parallel planning is a good ground-breaking activity. We should not force professionals to change, but we do need to encourage growth and reasonable adaptations to address the problems of fragmentation.

3. The nature of curriculum requirements. School curriculums vary in terms of how subjects are presented at each grade level and the flexibility in the school philosophy. A program where there are similar requirements for social studies and English might be able to foster an interdisciplinary unit more readily than one where there are great disparities. Sometimes, school requires participation in annual events that can be transformed into more powerful experiences with a short interdisciplinary unit, such as a school trip to a neighboring city or an environmental center. Curriculum designers should not make arbitrary decisions about which subject matter lends itself best to interdisciplinary work. Thoughtful consideration must be given to the best way to address school curriculum requirements and at the same time enliven the course of study.

## Combining Options

In my experience, school districts that use a combination of design options manifest the greatest success and the least fragmentation in their programs. Interdisciplinary designs should not be an all-or-nothing proposition. The following are examples of how a few schools have used varying formulas to meet the needs of their students and adapt effectively to their institutions. To demonstrate the use of the options, Figures 2.2-2.4 show schedules of three different interdisciplinary programs.

## Figure 2.2
## Integrating Elementary Science and Social Studies

| | 9:00–10:15 | 10:20–11:30 | 11:30–12 | 12:00–12:30 | 12:30–1:20 | 1:20–2:15 | 2:15–2:40 |
|---|---|---|---|---|---|---|---|
| FRI | Writers Workshop | MATH on Interdisc. Unit | Chorus/Instrumental Music | Lunch | Interdisciplinary Unit | | Library |
| THURS | Literature on Interdisc. Unit | Special Subjects (Music, Art, P.E.) | MATH Folders | Lunch | Interdisciplinary Unit (Emphasis on Science and Social Studies) | | Family Life |
| WEDN | Language Arts | MATH | Health Unit | Lunch | Science | Social Studies | Instrumental Music/Chorus |
| TUES | Literature on Interdisc. Unit | Special Subjects (Music, Art, P.E.) | MATH Folders | Lunch | Science | Social Studies | Library Study Skills |
| MON | Language Arts | MATH | Writers Workshop | Lunch | Physical Education | Interdisc. Unit | Family Life |

## Figure 2.3
## Integrating a Middle School Schedule

|  | | | | | | |
|---|---|---|---|---|---|---|
| MON | Interdisc. Team Academics | Physical Education | Lunch | Arts Team | Foreign Language | Science Lab |
| TUES | Math | Science and Lab | Lunch | Humanites Team | Instrum. Music/Band | Study Hall |
| WEDN | Interdisc. Team Academics / Math | Arts Team | Lunch | Physical Educ. / Family Life/Health | Study Hall | Math |
| THURS | Science | Humanities Team | Lunch | Physical Educ. / Family Life/Health | Foreign Language | Study Hall |
| FRI | Interdisc. Team Academics / Math / Science | Arts Team | Lunch | Interdisc. Team Academics | Instrum. Music/Band | Math |

**Figure 2.4**
**9th Grade Humanities Program***

| | A | B | C | D | E | F | G | H |
|---|---|---|---|---|---|---|---|---|
| | | | | | | HUMANITIES | | |
| FRI | | | | | | English/Social Studies Teachers | " | Art Teacher |
| THURS | | | | | | " | " | Music Teacher |
| WEDN | | | | LUNCH | | " | " | Art Teacher |
| TUES | | | | | | " | " | Music Teacher |
| MON | | | | | | " | " | Art Teacher |

*Classes in periods A-E are on traditional time schedule.

The elementary schedule in Figure 2.2 shows a program ~~where~~ *in which* the teacher presents an integrated science and social studies unit in an afternoon block. On Tuesday and Thursday, the reading program is based on literature that supports the integrated unit. On Friday afternoons, the grade level team has an interdisciplinary unit based on a theme that is relevant to young children and also meets the demands of some of the state requirements. This schedule was a collaborative effort of central office personnel and teachers.

The middle school in Figure 2.3 illustrates that certain subjects will be taught in a complementary fashion, such as the humanities. Other areas will remain as strictly discipline based such as the math block. Of great interest here is the integration of the arts areas, which had been taught in quarterly bites with one art form per quarter. Ownership in this design is widespread because the teachers planned and piloted various aspects of the schedule over a two-year period. This is a variation on the house model where the four academic areas do the day-to-day budgeting of time among themselves. These academic houses are committed to one interdisciplinary unit per semester.

The high school is often the most rigid institution in a school district, with strict time structures and state requirements for graduation. But Figure 2.4 shows that there can be some flexibility. In this school, humanities projects are taught in back-to-back time blocks. The principal was able to schedule the art and music teachers with an open period to participate in these blocks. Elective courses offered at this high school reflect the faculty's interdisciplinary orientation. High school teachers frequently complain about how time constraints inhibit practice. But at this school, the success of the humanities schedule has spurred the science, math, and technology departments to rethink how they might integrate their subjects.

\*   \*   \*

The purpose of this chapter is to walk through the choices available for integration. To avoid the trap of the polarity issue, school leaders need to consider the different degrees of change that are feasible in their school systems. The continuum of options has proven a very useful tool for perpetuating the change process in an intelligent and reflective fashion as planners weigh their options with care.

There is no right or wrong choice for integration, only a range of options with distinct advantages and disadvantages. Your task is to diagnose the needs and possibilities of your school and prescribe the combination that will best serve your students. In order to assist you in this set of choices, David Ackerman in Chapter 3 presents criteria that wrestle with curriculum, pragmatic, personal, and political considerations when designing programs that espouse integration.

# 3

# Intellectual and Practical Criteria for Successful Curriculum Integration

## David B. Ackerman

THIS CHAPTER AIMS TO PROVIDE A FRAMEWORK FOR TEACHERS AND CURRICU-
lum developers deliberating over whether to adopt a curriculum integration approach for some portion of their instructional program. The
framework consists of two overarching questions and some criteria
that can be used to answer them:

    1. Does it make intellectual sense to integrate certain parts of the
curriculum?

    2. Does it make practical sense, all things considered?

    To answer these questions, teachers and curriculum developers
need to test the interdisciplinary option against a set of conditions or
criteria. Among possible intellectual criteria is that knowledge gained
in one subject strengthens the understanding of concepts in other
subjects. Among possible pragmatic criteria are the anticipated attitudes of key individuals and groups—fellow teachers, parents, the
principal—toward what may be regarded as an atypical form of program organization. It is not always pedagogically sensible to intercon-
nect disparate pieces of the curriculum. Even when doing so might
seem beneficial, it is not always practically feasible. However, the

promise of enhancing the meaningfulness and impact of instruction should not be dismissed lightly. In the right circumstances, it the best choice for teachers and students. A number of pertinent intellectual and pragmatic criteria are presented below, first in general terms and then through discussion of two "real-world" examples.

## Intellectual Criteria

Curriculum integration certainly has a strong rhetorical appeal (could an enlightened educator really be against aiming to help students achieve a coherent view of things?), but can the idea withstand critical scrutiny?

Sometimes clearly not. Consider what Jacobs in Chapter 1 calls the "potpourri" and "polarity" problems. In the former, students are offered a sampling of thematically related experiences from different disciplines but are not guided to see how the diverse bits of knowledge form a coherent view of the topic. With the "polarity problem," the teacher or curriculum designer has adopted such an "antidisciplinary" attitude that vital discipline-based concepts are ignored or trivialized rather than enlarged through multidisciplinary connections.

Being aware of these pitfalls, let's identify a desirable set of criteria for an integrated curriculum. Imagine that a curriculum development team has selected a topic, concept, or "organizing center" that cuts across two or more disciplines; has used brainstorming to generate a set of prospective curriculum elements; and has sketched a potentially workable instructional sequence. Before investing the considerable effort required to produce such a curriculum (and to deal with numerous practical hurdles), the development team wants to feel more confident that a multidisciplinary or "integration" approach really makes sense for the topic they want to pursue.

Four criteria, intrinsic to the ideal of interdisciplinary education, can be used to guide the team's deliberation. Imagine these four criteria as a series of tests to be applied to the proposal under consideration. Depending on their evaluation of the results of these tests, the curriculum developers will decide to proceed or go back to the drawing board.

## Validity Within the Disciplines

Let's assume, again, that brainstorming has identified concepts within each discipline that pertain to a proposed interdisciplinary theme. It may be the case, however, that for one or more of the subjects being considered, the relevant concepts are not significant to the school curriculum for a particular year or in general. A case in point is the theme of kites, suggested in a monograph on interdisciplinary education in the middle school. The unit revolving around this theme would have science students learn about the aerodynamics of flight, social studies students inquire into the history and social significance of kite flying, English students compose "lofty" poetry, math students estimate altitude, and so on. But while these examples suggest how each subject *could* relate to the central theme, they leave open the question of whether each subject *should* devote a portion of instructional time to the interdisciplinary project. If the history of kite flying, for instance, is not considered an important topic in the social studies curriculum, and if teaching it can only be done by giving short shrift to topics considered more important, then social studies teachers will naturally be reluctant to endorse the interdisciplinary proposal. Validity within the disciplines requires teachers representing each discipline to verify that the concepts identified are not merely *related* to their subjects but are *important* to them.

## Validity For the Disciplines

Now let's assume that some concepts have been identified that are considered important to two or more subjects. The question then arises: Why stick them together in a multidisciplinary unit or course? Admittedly the concepts are related to a common theme, but so what? Might the "theme" be little more than verbal window dressing?

On the other hand, perhaps the prospects are not so meager. It might be the case, for example, that by comparing a concept from one subject with an analogous one from another subject, the student might actually learn these concepts *better* than if they had been taught separately. If this were so, a multidisciplinary approach might be *mutually beneficial* to teachers bent on pursuing their own subject goals. To the extent that it actually enhances the learning of discipline-based concepts, a multidisciplinary approach can be said to have validity for the disciplines.

To illustrate this criterion, let's compare a questionable curriculum possibility with a more promising one. The dubious example I have in mind is "cycles." On the surface, it looks exciting. Brainstorming might elicit all sorts of cycles in science (water and carbon dioxide cycles, Krebs' urea and citric acid cycles, and, of course, life cycles); cycles in history (e.g., Vico's and Toynbee's); cyclic groups, cyclic functions, and cyclic algorithms in mathematics; and the mythological cycle of birth, death, and rebirth in literature. The realm of associations is wide, and the concepts cited are important to their respective subject disciplines. However, this concurrence of terms may not be educationally significant. For example, how would a student exploring the birth-death-rebirth motif in Dickens' *A Tale of Two Cities* benefit from dragging in cosines or FOR NEXT loops? And while life cycles in biology and history may indeed be synergistic constructs, are the periodicities of citric acid and civilization mutually illuminating? Dimly, at best, it would appear.

A more promising example is the concept of "evidence," which I discuss briefly here and David Perkins elaborates on in Chapter 6. For present purposes, let's begin by considering a noninterdisciplinary status quo. To teach their subject matter logically and persuasively, science teachers talk to their students about the empirical data that underlie textbook knowledge; history teachers acknowledge the importance of archival records, eyewitness accounts, and the like; English teachers exhort their classes for textual evidence for their interpretations; and geometry teachers ask, "Beginning with just these few axioms, what can we prove?" But, while the concept of "evidence" is thus "in" the curriculum of these four subjects, the standard, discipline-centered instructional approach takes little or no notice of this coincidence. In a more dynamic scenario, a team of teachers decides to orchestrate a series of lessons in which students will compare and contrast the nature of evidence across the curriculum. This pedagogical strategy is based on the belief that students may grasp the distinctive features of scientific and other kinds of knowledge *better* by juxtaposing the perspectives of the different disciplines than by encountering them in isolation. From the individual teacher's perspective, the collaborative effort is not altruistic; the science teacher, for example, is betting that students will understand science better with the interdisciplinary approach than without it. A team effort is beneficial to teachers and students when it helps students achieve a better grasp of related concepts from different subjects by examining each one through multiples lenses.

## Validity Beyond the Disciplines

Thus far, the case for or against curriculum integration has been made in relation to the viewpoint of the separate disciplines, the achievement of whose goals may be enhanced if cross-curricular connections illuminate important subject-based ideas. Valid curriculum integration thus assembles a number of "parts" from different subjects, with the hope that students will learn the parts better in the process of exploring the interrelationships among them. But an integrated curriculum generally has, besides the disciplinary parts, some organizing center or theme or "hub"—"evidence," for example—to which they are connected. This central idea itself may be valuable for students to think about and to assimilate into their way of looking at the world. Alternatively, the power may derive from the interplay of the disciplines in illuminating complex phenomena. In either case, students can learn not only the usual concepts (and perhaps learn them better), but they can also get a metaconceptual bonus—a "powerful idea," a cross-cutting idea, a perspective on perspective taking, a dimension of experience—that may be of great value.

Is "cycles" such a dimension? Perhaps, but it might be difficult to make a convincing case. (The generalization that "in various realms, repeated sequences of events occur" connects but does not enlighten.) Middle school students might have a lot of fun with the topic of kites, but its validity doesn't really soar beyond the disciplines. In section III, we discuss two examples of organizing ideas that have the power to develop a sensibility incorporating and transcending those of the component subjects. One, Humanities, develops in students an awareness of how history, literature, art, and music can together illuminate the story of civilization. The other, Science/Technology/Society, highlights the vital interplay of epistemological, technical, moral, and political issues in contemporary society. In both cases, specific subject matter content is sketched on a canvas that compellingly transcends subject matter bounds. Insofar, then, as valuable interdisciplinary concepts are learned, and insofar as "the whole is greater than the sum of its parts," an integrated curriculum may have validity beyond the disciplines.

## Contribution to Broader Outcomes

In addition to imparting particular understandings within and beyond the disciplines, interdisciplinary education may help shape the learner's overall approach to knowledge. Students may become more skilled at and comfortable with flexible thinking and with adopting multiple points of view, for example. They may become more adept at generating analogies and metaphors, may comprehend them better, and may better understand their limitations. The strengths and limitations of the disciplines themselves may be more clearly grasped as well as the artificiality of sorting knowledge into separate "departments." Students may also come to *value* such skills and understandings: to thrill at interweaving diverse ideas and to shudder at discourse comprised of shreds and patches. Teachers or curriculum developers may hope that the intellectual values implicit in interdisciplinary education simply "rub off," but they may also build into their instructional plans explicit identification, modeling, and discussion of the desired habits of mind; activities designed to apply concepts beyond the scope of the particular unit or course; and even some means of evaluating the impact of the program on student attitudes toward knowledge. In any case, in deliberating over whether to adopt an interdisciplinary program, it is legitimate to assess its potential contribution to the development of desirable intellectual dispositions, and, more broadly, to the development of the person.

# Practical Criteria

Interdisciplinary curriculums are not simply intellectual edifices; they must occur within the realities of school time and space. Coordinating both the concepts and the people requires a determined effort, and even when there is a will, there may not be a practically effective way. While most of the criteria discussed below are pertinent to any curriculum change, they are especially salient for curriculum integration because of the complexity of the undertaking. Like the intellectual criteria, these pragmatic ones can be viewed as a series of tests to be applied to an interdisciplinary proposal that on curriculum grounds appears to be highly promising.

### "Nuts and Bolts"

Three essential practical considerations are time, budget, and schedule.

Time is required for curriculum development. Subject matter research may be necessary because an interdisciplinary approach places familiar material in a new light, raises new questions, or involves content that the teacher has not previously presented. Specific lessons and activities need to be planned. New tests need to be written or old ones modified. Additional time is needed for communication and coordination with colleagues, both during curriculum planning and development and after the actual program has begun. Extra time will also be required to teach students the interdisciplinary aspects of the curriculum, the curricular connections.

A budget must be available to support curriculum development, staffing, and acquisition of materials. If pertinent commercial materials are unavailable, the cost of hiring teachers to develop their own materials may be prohibitive. If the net result of involving more than one teacher in a course is a lower pupil-teacher ratio than normal, the added staffing cost may loom as an insuperable barrier.

The schedule is a factor on two accounts. Students and teachers must be scheduled so they are available for each other as required by the design of the course. Also, there ideally should be common planning time for the teachers. While these sorts of considerations may not be too difficult to accommodate in relation to the interdisciplinary program itself, competing needs of other programs may supersede.

A brief example may help to illustrate these nuts and bolts concerns. A Foreign Language Experiences program I am familiar with is designed to support a 6th grade Latin America curriculum by providing introductory lessons, twice weekly for 12 weeks, in Spanish language and culture. The itinerant Spanish teacher must be scheduled to teach all of the 6th graders in the district over the course of the year, and the classroom teachers must try to organize their social studies programs so that Latin America is being taught at the time of year when the Spanish teacher is on the scene. Obviously, these exigencies of the schedule are sometimes inconvenient. Moreover, adequate time has not yet been provided for coordinating the two curriculums (other curriculum development priorities have consumed the budget) or for the classroom teachers and Spanish teacher to communicate more than superficially with one another.

### "Political" Support

Because interdisciplinary education generally falls outside the norms of the culture of the school or school system, support from key individuals and groups will be necessary to launch and sustain the program. Such support is also essential if the proposed undertaking is costly or complex.

A department head, curriculum director, superintendent, or school committee may all be in the position to squelch an interdisciplinary education proposal or to contribute to its demise through inadequate support. Tradition-bound colleagues may discourage would-be interdisciplinary educators through peer pressure. An inhospitable community exerts its own forms of pressure. Parents in particular may discourage their children from signing up for interdisciplinary electives or may complain about nonelective programs that seem confusing or eccentric. (A 2nd grade teacher in our district who integrates the teaching of basic skills into a global education curriculum receives a few complaints each year about spelling lists that include words such as Parthenon.) Finally, as illustrated below, an interdisciplinary course may have the support of the relevant adults but fizzle because the students do not sign up.

A determined, carefully sequenced, support-building effort may be required to get a program off the ground or, especially if things do not go smoothly right away, to maintain it. The energy required for public relations and the likelihood of ultimate success must be calculated when deciding to pursue an interdisciplinary program.

### Personal Concerns

If not externally mandated, a decision by a teacher to venture into interdisciplinary realms is a personal one that may need to overcome any of a number of kinds of resistance. The sheer effort required—intellectually, practically, or both—may be daunting. Considerable anxiety may be felt over the prospect that, assurances to the contrary notwithstanding, one's subject matter "territory" will be compromised. As in any "marriage," attachment to an interdisciplinary team promises to bring into one's life, along with stimulation or even inspiration, a sizable set of not fully predictable vexations. A risk-taking venture offers the potential not just for professional renewal but for disheartening failure. Joy or travail? Collegiality or cantankerousness?

Expanded pedagogical repertoire or exposure of one's pedagogical limitations? Deeper understanding of one's own and other subjects or a loss of one's bearings? The payoff and risk of interdisciplinary education can both be high.

## The Criteria Exemplified: A Tale Of Two Programs

The criteria just presented can be grasped more vividly through examples of actual curriculums and of the teaching situations that embody them. In this section, two such examples are presented from my home district in Winchester, Massachusetts. Both are multi-disciplinary high school programs. The first, Humanities, brings together Western history, literature, art, and music into a single course offering presented collaboratively by four teachers, one from each of the four subject areas. It has successfully operated for 10 years.

The second example, "STS" (Science/Technology/Society) is a course struggling to be born. In 1987-88, it was approved by the school committee and included in the high school's schedule. Throughout the year, a team of three teachers, representing the science, social studies, and industrial arts/technology departments met to plan the curriculum. Unfortunately, because of insufficient enrollment, the course was not offered the following year (1988-89). As proposed, STS, like Humanities, was to have been a double period course for seniors. Students' difficulty with trying to fit a two-period course into their schedules was one of the reasons for STS's unsuccessful launching. Other factors will be noted below as we compare both of the programs in relation to the criteria presented earlier.

### Intellectual Criteria

Curriculum planning for both courses proceeded from the assumption that an interdisciplinary endeavor must be academically well grounded. In the case of Humanities, the enterprise is straightforward: The content comes directly from the disciplines (Western history, literature, art, and music) and the order is chronological. What makes the course extraordinary is the interplay among the subjects. Teachers presenting material from their own disciplines frequently allude to concepts presented by colleagues, for purposes of comparison, contrast, and reinforcement. Modeling an attitude of engagement and inquiry, a teacher occasionally "interrupts" a colleague to make a comment or raise a question. Assignments and examination questions require that students explore topics from multiple points of view and produce a coherent synthesis. Although a formal study has not been conducted, Humanities teachers are unanimous in the view that the multidisciplinary approach augments the learning of their individual subjects. They also feel that the intensive yearlong effort to approach the story of civilization through "multiple lenses" helps students develop a sensibility to history that transcends specific subject matter knowledge and a correspondingly sophisticated attitude toward knowledge in general. Abundant anecdotal evidence exists to support these beliefs.

In contrast to the Humanities program, which draws upon traditional course content, the STS undertaking has faced the daunting challenge of defining its subject matter. The assumption has been that each discipline needs to preserve its own integrity while contributing to the larger enterprise. This dual demand has necessitated new ways of thinking. In science, the traditional course sequence has been biology, chemistry, physics, and an Advanced Placement course. A challenging STS offering has come to be regarded as an exciting possibility for students who want a senior year alternative to Advanced Placement. But what science should be included in the STS course? There are many possibilities. What Winchester's curriculum development team has determined is that through study of issues such as acid rain, students should review and strengthen their understanding of pertinent concepts encountered in previous basic science courses; extend that basic knowledge as they acquire more specialized knowledge; and develop a deeper understanding of scientific research as it bears upon social issues, including the nature of the research, the results to date, the questions in need of further research, and the questions that are beyond the capacity of science to answer.

Social studies and industrial arts also have had to wrestle with content identification. In the case of social studies, the temptation was rejected to turn STS into another history course (because students all will have had three consecutive years of history). The plan is for the social studies teacher to present a capsule history of the issue and then focus on the politics of the decision-making process, including the role of interest groups, the interplay between formal and informal processes, the political uses of science, and the opportunities for individual citizen involvement. The industrial arts teacher will, among other things, present a weekly "technology lab" activity. The need to generate activities pertinent to the biological topics that will be covered has presented a considerable professional challenge, since the department's experience has been almost entirely in the physical science realm.

The individuals involved in STS curriculum development have thus carved out a program that will be grounded in what they believe to be valid science, social studies, and industrial arts education. As their Humanities colleagues do, the STS team expects that teachers will make cross-disciplinary references while presenting their own expert knowledge. Likewise, course projects and exams will require a synthesis of perspectives. During seminar days, teachers will remove their specialist's caps and participate along with students as "citizens," grappling with issues that affect everyone in the community. The "whole" that is greater than the sum of its parts is reasonably clear: It is the dynamic, consequential interplay of science, technology, and society, and it is regarded as an extremely valuable nexus of ideas to study. Less defined is the overall attitude toward knowledge that the course will promote among students, but the goals along these lines will certainly include developing a sense of appreciation for the complexity of real-world issues and the need to adopt multiple perspectives in order to achieve understanding.

## Practical Criteria

Although Humanities has come to flourish, the course initially had to surmount the same sorts of pragmatic hurdles that are frustrating the STS effort. The idea for a Humanities course was brought forward seven years before it was actually offered. The obstacles that had to be overcome included a music department in transition, an English department in turmoil, a new English director who demanded that 5 of the course's proposed 10 credits be in English, administrative concerns about budget (the course requires a higher staff-to-pupil ratio than the average), and about the failure of comparable programs in other communities. As a result of the persistence of the proponents and improved finances, the school committee voted to give the course a chance. With the course in its tenth year and flourishing, the initial trials and tribulations largely have been forgotten, and, as one veteran describes it, "everyone now claims to be a Founding Father."

The course has been such a resounding success that it has acquired its own mythos. Many regard it as the consummate learning experience in the high school. Prompted by the course's reputation for excellent teachers and for a degree of impact surpassing that of many college offerings, families plan long in advance to enroll their children. Statistically, the success story has been remarkable. While the school as a whole experienced a 40 percent enrollment decline during the 1980s, the Humanities enrollment doubled, necessitating a second section.

The program has certainly not been problem free, however. While most of the individuals who have taught Humanities have been outstanding teachers, there have been some weak links. A common planning period was scheduled several years ago, but this has gone by the boards as a result of scheduling difficulties. During some years, less serious students have had a dissipating effect on the classroom tone. Some staff members have seemed to resent the course's success. Friendly competition among the four teachers for time for their respective subjects is ongoing, and those who are weak advocates for their disciplines may lose some "turf." For the most part, though, the Humanities course has worked wonderfully.

The pragmatic side of the STS story reveals how many gears must mesh in order to get a multidisciplinary program going. The course grew out of the intuition that there is a valid place in the curriculum for a scientific-technology counterpart to Humanities, one that would summarize and transcend the subject-specific knowledge acquired in previous courses and, like Humanities, provide students with a senior year educational capstone. During exploratory discussions held over a period of approximately two years, considerable skepticism and excitement were expressed. When a sufficiently clear vision of the course finally coalesced, it was brought to the school committee, where it was enthusiastically embraced. Administrative support was solid at all levels. A promising teacher team was assembled, and they made considerable strides in curriculum development. When course registration forms were tallied, however, only four students had signed up; a promotional letter and a little arm twisting raised the number to nine, only half of the minimum needed to justify the expenditure. The course was therefore dropped.

The factors that contributed to the course's failure to draw students are important. The course demanded a commitment of a double period from seniors who may not have had room in their schedules. (The suggestion that the course be offered in a single period was rejected on budgetary grounds.) The course title and content were unfamiliar, and the course lacked the status (and grade-point average bonus) of advanced placement offerings. The only text deemed academically suitable was too difficult to allow the course to be offered at a "middle" ability level, thereby substantially narrowing the potential audience. Concerns by some individuals that the science content was insufficiently substantial resulted in a less than vigorous promotional effort within that department.

This year STS is being offered a second time, with one significant alteration in design. The course will be scheduled seven periods a week during one semester and eight periods a week during the other semester, neatly dovetailing with the required physical education program, which meets, respectively, three and two periods a week. With the double period design of the previous year, STS and PE would have consumed three periods in a seven-period day; under the current modification, only two periods will be required, and the potential for conflicts with other courses will be greatly reduced. With these few alterations and a full public relations campaign, perhaps STS will succeed.

\*     \*     \*

While it unquestionably has high rhetorical appeal, curriculum integration presents daunting challenges to those who would like to see it more widely embraced as an alternative or counterpart to subject-based curriculum. In this chapter, a set of intellectual and practical criteria for successful curriculum integration has been presented and described. The criteria can be used as a series of "tests" for cross-disciplinary ideas under consideration. And they can serve as a basis for discarding alluring but shallow or unworkable ideas, for revising ones that don't quite measure up but have potential, or for validating conceptions that with a lot of dedication and a little bit of luck can have an enormously positive impact. With its promise of unifying knowledge and modes of understanding, interdisciplinary education represents the pinnacle of curriculum development.

# 4

# Descriptions of Two Existing Interdisciplinary Programs

**Heidi Hayes Jacobs**

As WE DISCUSS CRITERIA FOR DETERMINING THE NATURE OF AND NEED FOR interdisciplinary curriculum, it is timely to examine two programs that applied Ackerman's guidelines. Whenever teachers attempt to create an innovation, the change process inevitably spills into other areas of school life. The following sagas written by an observer of an elementary team in Elizabeth, Colorado, and a high school team in Newtown, Connecticut, inform us about the decision-making process in interdisciplinary planning in terms of the intellectual and practical criteria discussed in the previous chapter. But perhaps even more telling are the personal voices of these curriculum designers, which bring reality to our examination of models, guidelines, and considerations.

I believe those of you who are engaged in bringing curriculum integration to your school setting will find these two program descriptions validating. We can identify with the struggles and satisfactions of professionals determined to address a need by changing their curricular practice.

## A Year-Long High School Humanities Course

*Joyce Hannah, William Manfredonia, and John Percivalle*[1]

Newtown is an affluent, western Connecticut bedroom community of about 21,000 people, many of whom commute to jobs in southern Connecticut and nearby New York.

Newtown High School's year-long humanities class, which meets every day for 44 minutes, gives juniors and seniors the option of receiving credit in either art, English, or music. The three team teachers of this course are specialists in each of those disciplines. They share a mutual preparation period each day, which they have found to be a necessity for ensuring quality team teaching.

### The Curriculum

Our humanities curriculum places a strong emphasis on the process of learning as well as content. Students not only study *about* art, music, and literature, they *make* art, music, and literature in a setting that encourages cooperative learning and higher-order thinking skills.

We have integrated several behavioral concepts into a specific content unit on the Middle Ages.

1. Students achieve *cooperative learning* through process writing, group tests, and group projects in which they can take class leadership roles.

2. Students also know they have a *responsibility to share their learning* with others in the class, school, and community, and they are given chances to do so. We want our students to realize that there is a valuable learning environment outside the school itself. In addition to taking students out of the classroom for museum and gallery visits and performances, we regularly invite guest speakers and performers (including some from within our own building) to visit the humanities class. Because we have no textbook for humanities, our coursework is evolutionary and often depends on the class make-up, community and district performances, current issues, and speaker

---

[1]William Manfredonia is serving as Newtown High School's interim principal; Joyce Hannah and John Percivalle are two of the three humanities team teachers.

availability. Once, when a touring Shakespearian group from England performed at a nearby university, we scrapped our planned approach and instead built a unit around Macbeth involving Faustian and tragic hero archetypes.

3. We emphasize a *multisensory, experience-oriented* curriculum that encourages creative problem solving. Students are required to become involved in hands-on projects that integrate unit concepts. Not only do students answer questions and investigate ideas, they also shape their own questions and projects. Such methods demonstrate that in most cases there is no one right answer. Students' journals and class discussions of the process aspect of the course provide ongoing self- and course assessment.

The humanities course attempts to introduce the relationship of western themes to nonwestern cultures by investigating such ideas as myth, hero, creation, and space, where global parallels can be established. The questions we ask students—What makes a person a hero? What are the ramifications of man's manipulation of space? What is the ongoing significance of myth-making? What is the importance of understanding one's cultural heritage?—cannot help but include discussions of cultures other than our own. Such questions also force the instructors to cross cultural boundaries as well as the boundaries of traditional disciplines. Consequently, we find ourselves teaching history, social studies, geography, art, literature, music, dance, religion, philosophy, math, and science!

An example of how we approach our class is seen in our study of the Middle Ages. Students read and studied *Sir Gawain and the Green Knight* in terms of Joseph Campbell's hero cycle. References were made to 20th century heroes, including characters from the movie *Star Wars*. Students also looked at *Gawain* as a mirror of the courtly and religious codes of the medieval period. Their study of courtly love poetry was followed by a lesson in calligraphy and the development of writing up to the Renaissance. After viewing illuminated manuscripts at the Beinecke Rare Book Library at Yale, each student wrote a courtly love poem and hand lettered it in the style of the period. These love poems were secretly sent to other class members on Valentine's Day.

Students conducted individualized research projects on such topics as the role of science and scientific inquiry in the Middle Ages, feudal hierarchy, knighthood, the role of women in medieval society,

Dante's levels of hell/heaven, stained glass, Marco Polo, and alchemy. They worked in groups of two or three to research and prepare class presentations that required audio-visual components and participatory tactics. One group constructed a mushroom-outlined fairy ring from which they acted out various medieval legends involving supernatural beliefs. Others investigated geography, especially the role of Marco Polo's journeys. They also discussed the influence of Islam under the reign of Suleyman. A huge student-made map was used to show the scope of Islam and how European power centers were forced away from the Mediterranean. To reinforce the idea visually and tactilely, students representing various cities and personages actually sat on a 10' x 30' map of Europe.

The class completed peer evaluation sheets and took notes for developing questions for the closure activity, a game of Jeopardy in which the answers were the names, places, and dates the students had been learning. Tests were devoted to the larger conceptual issues.

After viewing Macaulay's "Cathedral," students studied the art and architecture of the European Middle Ages. A guest speaker from the Newtown High School staff showed slides of Romanesque and Gothic structures. The class took a field trip to the Cloisters, an authentic medieval structure (now part of the Metropolitan Museum of Art) overlooking the Hudson River. Our guide had us sing in one of the chapels to demonstrate its resonance and asked the students to work together with building blocks to create Gothic and Romanesque arch structures. Showing us the Unicorn tapestries, he noted the parallels between symbols in it and in our poetry, and he described life in a monastic setting. Best of all, students got firsthand knowledge about their recent class presentations.

We also studied monophonic music, Gregorian chant, and polyphony. Those who read music taught small groups of their peers so that everyone could write at least a small piece of polyphonic text. We invited the Ensemble for Early Music from Lincoln Center to be guests for this aspect of the unit. All Newtown High School classes were encouraged to attend performances throughout the day to hear authentic medieval and early Renaissance music sung and played on facsimiles of period instruments. The ensemble explained the music, lyrics, instruments, and milieu for both sacred and secular pieces.

Bergman's film *The Seventh Seal* was shown as an example of a knight's quest. The influence of the plague and the transition into the

Renaissance were represented by Antonius Bloch's questioning of the Church's dogma about good and evil.

We have not been successful with all of our students. Some never adjust to a learning environment that is alien in many ways to the one they've experienced for 10 years, one that demands independent thinking, full hands-on participation, cooperation with peers, and ownership of their education.

For other students, it has been the most exciting educational experience they have ever had. Others are reserving judgment. As one student said, "Don't ask me now what I've learned; give me a year and ask me then."

### Applying Ackerman's Criteria to the Project

*Curriculum Criteria.* Our humanities course encourages students to think in an interdisciplinary manner, a skill that gives them a framework for synthesizing their educational experiences. This way of looking at the world is the whole that proves, in the long run, to be greater than the sum of the parts. Already we find our students asking,"Where does this fit?" rather than "Why do we need to know this?" Knowledge gained in an interdisciplinary environment is mutually reinforcing. When subjects are taught in isolation, "accumulation" of knowledge is the focus; an integrated curriculum demands higher-order connection making and synthesis that promote real, long-term understanding.

One of the most valuable "broader outcomes" of this approach has been in the area of cooperative learning. By its very definition, "interdisciplinary" implies cooperation, not only among academic disciplines but among people. An emphasis on cooperative learning, in which students of varying abilities and talents learn from one another, has been a natural outgrowth of our program. Students who read music help teach those who don't; students with visual art experience guide their peers in the use of materials and techniques; and in writing, the process approach, which stresses revision motivated by peer feedback, again allows students to teach students. The implication, learned by example in the course, is that learning is most valuable when it is shared to benefit others.

*Pragmatic Criteria.* Unless serious consideration is given to potential pragmatic difficulties, the pedagogical benefits of a new program cannot be realized. We have found time to be one of the most critical areas requiring administrative support. At first glance, we expected that time would not be a problem since there are three teachers to share the load. To the contrary, we have found that team teaching an interdisciplinary course compounds time demands. More time is needed for:

- reaching consensus on curriculum plans and criteria for tests and grading,
- subject matter research because we always find ourselves teaching new material,
- planning lessons that use untraditional approaches,
- arranging for field trips, guest speakers, and special events,
- the networking that is required to make contacts with other staff members, community resources, and parents who can help expand the learning environment,
- course evaluation, which involves ongoing meetings with administrators,
- professional development (research, workshops, and visitations) to keep up with interdisciplinary education, and
- public relations to maintain support for an innovative program.

Although adjustments have been made, we still struggle with the constrictions of an 8-period day in which humanities meets for only 44 minutes. Forty-four minutes of daily instructional time has proven especially restrictive in a program that stresses broadening the educational environment through field trips and guest speakers in an experiential approach that often involves extensive set-up and take-down time for hands-on activities and student performances. Even though the course encompasses three disciplines, it is considered a single course for which students receive credit in just one subject area. A better approach would be to double or even triple the class periods and allow students to earn credits in more than one discipline. A larger block of time would open up many more instructional possibilities.

*Political Criteria.* Our humanities course exists in a politically supportive environment. We have attempted to foster involvement and trust among our colleagues by offering them opportunities to participate in a clearly articulated program. Many of our "guest" presenters come from our own faculty. Territorial anxieties have therefore been dispelled. Staff members regularly cover classes for teachers who give time to the program. The course has encouraged cooperation, sharing, and increased communication schoolwide.

Surprisingly, we have found that students are the slowest to adjust. Many students have initial difficulties with the humanities class because they are so inured to a compartmentalized learning style. Some are threatened by participatory learning and find it difficult to take risks. In a course that attempts to de-emphasize grades, many students are too grade oriented and accustomed to working in only a competitive setting to take full advantage of the opportunities to share and learn from one another.

Students who have been successful memorizing material have difficulty adapting to a course that demands independent, creative thinking and values asking questions as highly as answering them.

Too often, we find this single dose of interdisciplinary education to be too little, too late. This is one of the major drawbacks of the program and has prompted us to investigate alternatives, such as the school-within-a-school concept, to bring interdisciplinary education to a greater number of students over a long term.

Fortunately, many students have been caught up in the excitement of the program and have blossomed within the freedom they initially found threatening. In fact, one of the "humanizing" benefits of the program has been that students who have achieved in a predominantly left-brained system have come to appreciate others who have not achieved in this same setting, but nevertheless have insights and abilities to share.

*Personal Criteria.* In isolation, the humanities course will remain an interesting aberration, but if it can become a catalyst for restructuring an often anachronistic educational system, its far-reaching benefits can be realized. The course has shown that with greater flexibility in scheduling and emphasis on collaboration, teachers can become creative problem solvers. Students benefit from stimulating programs, while teachers gain professionally from a process that allows them to think, make decisions, and act on their visions.

# A Two-Week K-6 Interdisciplinary Unit

*Judith C. Gilbert*

Elizabeth, Colorado, is a rural area 40 miles southeast of Denver. The location and small-town atmosphere attract people who work in the Denver metropolitan area, and there has been a 10 percent yearly increase in student population over the past three-and-a-half years. Sixty percent of the families in the community have children in school.

I met the Running Creek Elementary School's 1st grade teachers when the state department of education's science consultant and I worked with them to set up a two-week interdisciplinary unit using a model we had developed. Now, five years later, the 1st grade team has increased from three to five teachers and progressed to an all-encompassing philosophy that looks at a concept in its entirety and then figures out how the district curriculum can be taught in that context. The teachers estimate that 80 percent of their year is now spent in interdisciplinary work. Their success and enthusiasm has captured the interest of the entire school faculty to the extent that a two-week K-6 interdisciplinary space project involving every teacher and student in the school has become an annual event.

## The Curriculum

*The first interdisciplinary unit.* Dinosaurs was the first theme chosen for an interdisciplinary unit because of its high interest level, its correlation to existing curriculum (rocks and minerals, plant eaters vs. meat eaters), and the availability of materials. Following the Essentials Integrated Curriculum Model developed by consultants at the Colorado Department of Education, the teachers brainstormed ideas for activities, sequenced them, and mapped them according to the subject areas, skills, and processes that are introduced and practiced.

A major concept the teachers wanted to cover concerned the size of dinosaurs. One of the more artistically talented teachers drew a full-sized outline of a dinosaur on the school's parking lot, and the number of children who could fit inside the dinosaur was calculated. When it was discovered that the dinosaur was two school buses long, two buses were moved back to back inside the dinosaur outline. The bus drivers made a platform that fit from the end of one bus into the other, and the 1st graders moved through the vehicles, into the head of the dinosaur and out the tail. The students then determined that a dinosaur was 10 children tall. To illustrate this fact, 10 children's silhouettes were traced vertically on a roll of butcher paper. The school's custodian climbed the fire escape to the roof and dropped the paper off the top of the three-story building. When it was apparent that the paper was longer than the school was tall, students understood that a dinosaur could easily look over the building.

To illustrate how knowledge about dinosaurs is discovered, another teacher cooked chickens for several weeks, carefully preserving the bones. The teachers filled milk cartons with layers of sand, gravel, and dirt, burying the bones within the layers. Before the students made their "archaeological dig," they practiced on chocolate chip cookies, attempting to remove the chips without pulverizing the cookie. The importance of having the correct tools (toothpicks) became apparent. The children also made their own fossils.

Another concept that was difficult for 1st graders to grasp was the idea of how long ago the dinosaurs lived. An activity designed to illustrate this concept was carried out on the school playground. After completing timelines identifying historical events and people (Christ, the pilgrims, Columbus, Lincoln), students formed a single line and took steps backward to illustrate how long ago an event occurred. The time their parents were born was measured by one step, another step their grandparents, until the children identifying the time of the dinosaurs had walked backward two blocks (the length of a football field).

The culminating activity was a trip to the Denver Museum of Natural History. It was intriguing to see a group of adults huddled around a 1st grader explaining the dioramas, murals (sometimes referred to as "diarrheas" and "urinals"), and artifacts on display.

Several outcomes were noted at the completion of the unit: a significant drop in 1st grade absenteeism; greater student and parent enthusiasm and involvement; better student and teacher attitudes toward learning and school; more cooperation among participating teachers; and student development of lifelong learning skills such as responsibility and self-direction, independent study, research, and time management.

*The second interdisciplinary unit.* The following year, the teaching team included two of the original three teachers and added three more because of a dramatic 16 percent increase in students. Because of continued interest in interdisciplinary teaching, the faculty voted to develop a unit on space for the whole school. Space was chosen because of the interest generated by the Challenger tragedy and because of its relevance to world issues and geography. One of the teachers later reflected that the unit seemed to serve as a catharsis for some of the children who had watched the Challenger explosion on television and continued to be disturbed by its images.

As a group, the teachers brainstormed a flow of concepts and then broke them into sequential focusing points for each grade level. The grade-level teachers then worked together to develop units around the focusing points. "Special" teachers—music, art, physical education, computers, and library—travelled from group to group to see what they might contribute. After the units were written, a representative from each grade level and the special teachers formed a Space Committee charged with coordinating and scheduling all the activities for the two-week unit. It was necessary to find a common ground between teachers who were comfortable with the format and others who weren't. The planning time that involved all of the teachers eventually helped to generate mutual respect and the ability to recognize different strengths in different people.

To begin the unit, a 6th grade entry was chosen for the school space flag, and a 2nd grader's slogan, "Step into the Future," was chosen as the motto. In special ceremonies, the school was renamed "Cape Elizabeth," and rooms began to sport signs reading Waste Disposal Unit, Galley, Mess Hall, Data Base, and Fitness Chamber. The parent organization rented a moonwalk attraction from a local carnival owner so that students could experience the sensation and problems of weightlessness. A local group of amateur parachutists was invited to "drop" in.

Kindergartners learned about the history of flight and went on a hot-air balloon ride. The 1st grade went through an astronaut training program that included the study of communication, weather, gravity, planets, and stars. The 2nd grade established a colony on the moon. The 3rd grade designed a space station and built a space capsule to experience "confinement day." The 4th grade studied the solar system and organized themselves into "crews" for further research on individual planets. The 5th grade established a new colony in space and, after relocation, charted the night skies, named the constellations, and created laws, a flag, and a planet anthem. The 6th grade designed and built a totally self-contained and life-supporting space ark. The only problem they encountered was that the ark was so big it had to be sawed in half to remove it from the classroom.

Several outcomes were noted following the all-school interdisciplinary space unit. The open house that year was so popular the hallways were crowded. Teachers had a greater appreciation of the work the 1st grade team had done (and continued to do) with their interdisciplinary units. The 3rd grade teachers recognized new avenues to reach kids and began planning their own units. Part of the 5th grade team began to work together in developing its own units. The negative attitudes of some of the teachers turned into significant support as they became active participants in this new perspective of their disciplines.

The 1st grade teachers continued to expand their repertoire: A Stone Soup unit based on the old folk tale taught that sharing is part of Thanksgiving. Early crafts, family needs, and early housing were explored, and a "rock" opera was presented. The Gift of the Five Senses unit came just before Christmas. Five packages containing candy canes, a kaleidoscope, teddy bears, a music box, and potpourri on a Christmas tree introduced this health-related unit. Children discovered the importance of each sense, increased their empathy and understanding of the handicapped, and learned how to take care of their five senses. A short April Fools unit was also planned, and in May dinosaurs stalked the halls once again.

*The present and future.* During the third year of the interdisciplinary work, the 1st grade teaching team—and they now continually refer to themselves as a team—taught the Stone Soup unit at Thanksgiving, the Gift of the Five Senses at Christmas, a one-week unit on stock shows and rodeos in January during the National Western Stock Show in Denver (including activities on judging animals, a field trip to the Silver Buckle working ranch, a chuck wagon dinner, and a stuffed animal pet store), the dinosaur unit in February, and the space unit in April.

Additional units are continually being developed. Last fall, when the Barnum and Bailey circus came to Denver, the 1st grade teachers taught a unit on the circus. They made the parts for a life-sized pink elephant and measured the children in relation to them. A bar chart was made to graph the results. They discovered that an elephant's trunk holds one and a half gallons of water, so they weighed that much water and then determined whether a child weighed more or less than the water. Everyone helped stuff the elephant with newspapers, and five mothers hung the elephant on the playground backstop to provide the backdrop for a circus show featuring ring masters, lion tamers, and muscle men, all appropriately costumed.

## The Effects of Interdisciplinary Teaching

The collegiality of the 1st grade teaching team has developed to the point that teachers may or may not be involved in developing new projects, depending on their time and level of energy. One of the teachers said she regards this respect for individual needs and wishes as one of the most appealing aspects of her teaching assignment.

For each interdisciplinary unit, the team has identified minimum exit requirements, and long-term outcomes are emphasized more than day-to-day requirements. Skills are taught deliberately, but not tied to drill and practice and textbook sequences. Application becomes paramount as skills are used over and over again in different contexts. Besides developing conceptual understandings of the various topics, the students have experienced the joy of learning, discovering, and understanding.

Other grade level teachers have noticed the hobbies and interests that the children are developing as a result of their work in a 1st grade interdisciplinary unit. The children seem to remember more, believe that what they have to contribute is important, and participate more fully in class activities. They accept differences and appreciate the strengths and talents of their classmates.

Among the teachers, more sharing is apparent, as is a sense of pride and accomplishment. The teachers, by their own evaluation, are more open to questions and have discovered that good teaching is not presenting information but "getting out of the way" of the students' learning.

Both students and teachers have a renewed interest and enthusiasm for school. Administrative and community support for the interdisciplinary work has substantially increased. The principal has applied for grants to further support the project; the superintendent has visited the program and shared ideas with teachers; and the community maintains active involvement in every phase of the projects.

Martin Marietta has provided space engineers to work with the students and has promised further involvement in future space study.

The teachers estimate that 164 hours of time is needed to develop a unit. This includes brainstorming, developing and sequencing activities, finding resources and materials, setting up speakers and field trips, researching the subject matter, teaching the unit, and monitoring student and teacher progress. The 1st grade team agrees that significantly more time and effort, particularly in finding materials for slower learners, are required to prepare the interdisciplinary units. They also believe that their beginning efforts were overplanned, but as they gained experience, planning was less time consuming because the philosophy behind interdisciplinary teaching makes minute-to-minute planning unnecessary.

The interdisciplinary work at Running Creek Elementary School has resulted in better student self-discipline, improved attendance (85 percent traditionally vs. 98 percent during the dinosaur unit), fewer visits to the school nurse, increased homework completion, and better attitudes toward school. Teachers are more creative, enthusiastic, and collegial; they use time more effectively and have developed personal and professional pride in their teaching. They're sharing with and supporting each other more, feeling less isolated, and creating a more relevant and flexible curriculum in tune with the needs and interests of the students and the community.

# 5

# The Interdisciplinary Concept Model: A Step-by-Step Approach for Developing Integrated Units of Study

## Heidi Hayes Jacobs

IT IS SUMMER. THE SCHOOL BOARD HAS ALLOCATED MONEY FOR A TEAM OF teachers to develop an interdisciplinary unit for implementation in the fall. Four teachers are in shorts and sneakers sitting around the table in the faculty room ready to write. But where do they begin? An interdisciplinary unit is not like a conventional curriculum writing project in the standard disciplines. It is easy to see why so many writing projects fall prey to the "potpourri problem" described in Chapter 1. The teachers do not have clear guidelines for interdisciplinary curriculum from their state education department, their school districts, or commercial publishers. Too often, the team sitting around the table feels insecure about writing the unit. They are asking themselves, "Where are we going to take our students?" In a sense, that is the ultimate design question curriculum makers should ask.

The Latin derivation for the word curriculum is "a course to run." We are planning a path with every curriculum experience we design. The creation of interdisciplinary paths takes more deliberation, for the courses to run have not been set by others and the possibilities seem limitless. The teachers' task is to shape and to clarify the unit of study to ensure success.

Presented here is a systematic approach to the development of interdisciplinary units at all levels of instruction. The framework remains consistent regardless of the age of the students. You will recognize the historical roots of this approach from such concepts as the integrated curriculum, core curriculum, webbing strategies, and inquiry techniques. The synthesis of these elements produces a functional alternative to the patchwork of interdisciplinary curriculums that frequently emerges from older concepts.

The central aim of this interdisciplinary model is to bring together the discipline perspectives and focus them on the investigation of a target theme, issue, or problem. It is titled the Interdisciplinary Concept Model (Jacobs and Borland 1986) because the hope is to encourage an understanding of the *concept* of interdisciplinarity as well. We want students to be conscious of the relationships among disciplines as they investigate the subject matter. The first task then is to select the topic.

## Step 1. Selecting an Organizing Center

The teachers begin by selecting an organizing center, which acts as the focus for curriculum development. The topic can be a theme, subject area, event, issue, or problem; however, certain criteria should be considered when determining the center.

An organizing center should neither be so general and all-encompassing that it is beyond the scope of a definitive investigation, nor should it be so narrow that it restricts the parameters of study. Conceptual topics lend themselves to study because they are by definition abstract. Concepts such as observations, patterns, light, revolution, humor, flight, pioneers, the future, and world hunger have proven highly effective as organizing centers. Students can grow enormously by taking a traditional subject area and looking at it through more complex perspectives. Teachers have stimulated more interest in mundane subjects in the standard curriculum by injecting an inter-disciplinary emphasis.

Events can also be highly effective organizing centers because of the many levels from which they can be explored. Events can include not only current news happenings but also historical and possible future occurrences, as well as events ongoing in the students' lives such as producing a play, writing a literary magazine, and finding a job. It is obviously important to select a topic that is relevant to students, interesting, and crosses discipline lines. Students can aid the process by helping select topics. Once a topic is selected, it must be broadened to provide a base for investigation from various points of view, as Perkins notes in Chapter 6. This need sets the purpose for Step 2.

## Step 2. Brainstorming Associations

To encourage the deliberate exploration of the theme from all discipline fields, teachers and students use a graphic device: a six-spoked wheel (see Figure 5.1). As the diagram shows, the organizing center for the topic or theme is the hub of the wheel. Each of the spokes is a discipline area. The disciplines represent standard school subjects: mathematics, language arts, social studies, the arts, humanities, philosophy, and science. Before brainstorming associations, it is vital that students are aware of the distinct characteristics of each of the six disciplines and that each discipline allows them to view the theme from a distinct perspective.

Now brainstorming begins. Brainstorming is an open-ended technique for generating ideas. Osborne (1963) notes that a brainstorming session produces a great quantity of ideas from which a better quality of ideas can be selected. He suggests four basic principles to encourage brainstorming:

a. Criticism is ruled out during the session.

b. "Free-wheeling" is encouraged. Spontaneous and unusual responses promote creativity.

c. A quantity of ideas are elicited. Evaluation will follow.

d. Combination and improvement are sought. Participants should attempt to join two or more ideas into another idea and to better proposed ideas (p. 156).

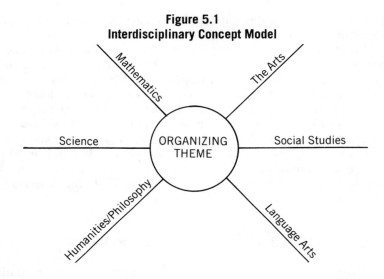

**Figure 5.1**
**Interdisciplinary Concept Model**

Before brainstorming in a group, individual participants should spend several minutes brainstorming on their own because this increases group productivity (Osborne 1963). Quiet, personal brainstorming for two minutes allows group members to get their juices flowing and truly helps the session.

The teachers and students are to brainstorm associations that relate to the organizing center in the hub. The associations may include questions, topics, people, ideas, and materials that relate to the central topic. The teacher jots down the associations under the discipline where an association might fall. For example, the name of a famous figure might fall under social studies and language arts.

Working on the wheel reveals areas that are not being covered and provokes interest in areas that might otherwise be ignored. It is likely that most people favor the orientation of certain disciplines. By bringing multiple perspectives to the foreground, participants are presented directly with alternative viewpoints. Certainly there are topics that may favor one or two disciplines more than others. Political events, for example, lend themselves to investigation through the social studies area. The aim is not to have an equal number of associations per discipline; rather, it is to promote the deliberate examination of the topic through all discipline perspectives. Figure 5.2 displays the first and second steps of unit development on the topic of flight. A few of the associations brainstormed by a group of 4th and 5th graders are shown as examples.

A high school unit on intelligence is displayed in Figure 5.3. Under each discipline spoke are examples of associations that evolved in the second brainstorming step. When these units were planned with groups of students, there were over 100 associations; however, for the sake of our discussion, only a few are highlighted. An advantage of this model is that from the start, students are reflecting on the organizing centers from each discipline viewpoint.

**5.2**
**Interdisciplinary Concept Model**
**A Unit on Flight—Steps 1 and 2**

PHILOSOPHY
Fight or Flight?
The ethics of airport noise
Why do we fly?

MATH
Angles for a smooth landing
Scale models of airport
Economics of flying, airfares, etc.

THE ARTS
Da Vinci's designs
Design Japanese kite
Films on Flight—
   Star Wars
Mobiles

FLIGHT

SCIENCE
Birds-flight patterns
Aerodynamics
Insects that fly
Space Flight
UFO's

LANGUAGE ARTS
Biographies: Wright Bros.
Amelia Earhardt
James Audubon
Flying heroes: Superman
Peter Pan
Icarus

SOCIAL STUDIES
History of flight
Compare social value of balloon, jet, etc.
Occupations in flight

# Figure 5.3
## Interdisciplinary Concept Model
## A Unit on Intelligence—Steps 1 and 2

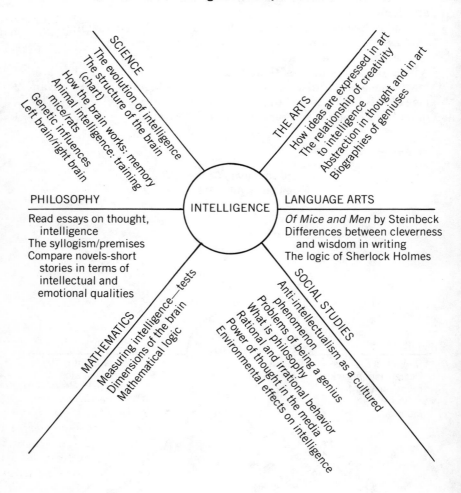

**SCIENCE**
The evolution of intelligence
The structure of the brain (chart)
How the brain works: memory
Animal intelligence: training mice/rats
Genetic influences
Left brain/right brain

**THE ARTS**
How ideas are expressed in art
The relationship of creativity to intelligence
Abstraction in thought and in art
Biographies of geniuses

**PHILOSOPHY**
Read essays on thought, intelligence
The syllogism/premises
Compare novels-short stories in terms of intellectual and emotional qualities

**INTELLIGENCE**

**LANGUAGE ARTS**
*Of Mice and Men* by Steinbeck
Differences between cleverness and wisdom in writing
The logic of Sherlock Holmes

**MATHEMATICS**
Measuring intelligence—tests
Dimensions of the brain
Mathematical logic

**SOCIAL STUDIES**
Anti-intellectualism as a cultured phenomenon
Problems of being a genius
What is philosophy
Rational and irrational behavior
Power of thought in the media
Environmental effects on intelligence

The questions and associations that result from the brainstorming set the stage for Step 3.

## Step 3. Establishing Guiding Questions to Serve as a Scope and Sequence

The third step of the model addresses the potpourri problem. This step takes the array of brainstormed associations from the wheel and organizes them. A structure for the unit of study will occur as a scope and sequence of guiding questions is developed. The questions are cross-disciplinary in nature and are analogous to chapter headings in a textbook. We would never give students a textbook without a table of contents that outlines the scope and the sequence of the book. The table of contents tells us not only what the book contains but what it does not contain. An interdisciplinary unit of study needs the same type of limits. We have to deal with real time constraints, and we have to give students the sequence of study and the reasons for it. Otherwise, we run the risk of simply delving haphazardly into an interesting theme.

In the two examples on flight and intelligence, the teachers considered general questions that moved from fundamental issues to more complex ones. The flight unit used these questions for a six-week period:

1. What flies? (This included not only the obvious animal and man-made things that fly, but ideas that fly, time flying, and runaways in flight.)
2. How and why do things in nature fly?
3. What has been the impact of flight on human beings?
4. What is the future of flight?

There are many ways that the teachers of the flight unit could have shaped their curriculum, but they chose these four questions as the range that seemed sensible to them. They created a scope and sequence and wrestled with the problem instead of leaping into activity design.

The high school team devised these questions to organize their study on intelligence.

1. What is intelligence?
2. How did human intelligence evolve?

3. How is intelligence measured?
4. Is intelligence a solely human quality?
5. How is creative intelligence expressed?

There are now guiding questions that should eventually be presented to students to introduce them to the unit of study. The questions are the framework for investigating the organizing center. Hopefully, they transcend discipline lines and provide the structure for the planners to write activities.

## Step 4. Writing Activities for Implementation

Once the guiding inquiry questions have been formulated, the means for exploring these questions must be developed. Activity design is the nuts and bolts of the unit of study; it tells us what students will be *doing* to examine the interdisciplinary organizing center. One of the guiding principles of effective planning is that teachers are able to encourage critical and creative thinking in their daily lesson plans. In a sense, we cue students about our expectations of them as thinkers in our daily assignments.

A model of cognition should guide activity design to ensure the cultivation of higher-level thought processes. Bloom's Taxonomy (1956) is the guideline for the flight unit and a creative problem-solving model frames the intelligence unit. A content-process matrix can aid in defining the task of activity planning, as shown in Figures 5.4 and 5.5. The rows in the matrix represent the guiding questions that structure the overall content of the unit. The columns represent the thinking processes to be emphasized in the activities planned. The examples in Figures 5.4 and 5.5 clarify how teachers can design a progression of activities derived from the brainstorming session. These are working drafts to show the overall design; refining the activities will follow. It is not necessary to develop one activity for each cell of the matrix; rather, the designer should look for the cumulative effect of the activities throughout the unit. For example, if the flight unit contains 80 percent of its activities on the first two levels of Bloom's Taxonomy, the message is clear: The unit will promote only recall of information. The matrix serves as a graphic picture of the actual design focus for thinking that is built into the interdisciplinary design.

**Figure 5.4**
**PROCESSES**
(Bloom's Taxonomy 1956)

| UNIT: Flight | KNOWLEDGE | COMPREHENSION | APPLICATION | ANALYSIS | SYNTHESIS | EVALUATION |
|---|---|---|---|---|---|---|
| 1. How does nature fly? | Identify birds' flight patterns | Recall principles of bird flight | Chart the movements of bird flight | Compare to man-made flying machines | | |
| 2. How and why do people fly? | List principles of aerodynamics | Translate these principles to: balloon jet hang-glider | Illustrate the principles as they apply to space flight | What are the historical reasons for change in flying preferences? Write in essay form | Create a new flying machine in blue-print | Appraise the machine's effectiveness |
| | | Read the biography of Lindburgh and Earhardt | List modern-day counterparts to these fliers | Compare similarities & differences between past and modern flight heroes | Write a biography of a fictional flying hero of the future | |

**Figure 5.5**
**PROCESSES/INQUIRY QUESTION MATRIX**
(Problem-Solving Model)

| UNIT: INTELLIGENCE | GATHERING DATA | ANALYZING THE DATA | DESIGN SOLUTIONS |
|---|---|---|---|
| 5. How can intelligence be measured? | Write a summary of the methods and considerations that psychologists and measurement experts use when designing tests. | Analyze the following tests for elementary students: WISC, Otis, Lennon, CTBS. List any areas that might prove problematic. Use items from the test to support your arguments. | Design an intelligence test based on behavioral characteristics for students in your class. It should predict success in the class. |
| 6. How has intelligence evolved? | Chart the evolution of animal and human intelligence on a timeline. Use illustrations when appropriate. | On the basis of what we know about the hemispheres of the brain, analyze the dominant hemispheres you use in home and school functions. | Design an anatomical diagram of the brain of human beings ten thousand years from now. You should be able to support any changes in the brain on the basis of past evolutionary trend. |

Teachers should employ a number of modalities and a variety of grouping patterns as they devise activities. The full gamut of instructional experiences can be incorporated into the design: Written, spoken, sculpted, danced, debated, or filmed outcomes are a handful of the types possible. To encourage both individual and cooperative learning, we can design activities that deliberately use dyads, triads, and large and small groups. The goal is to set up optimal conditions to support each day's activities.

Since our goal is for activities to reflect the full gamut of instructional possibilities—lecture, group projects, learning centers, discussion, research, or design—it is of primary importance that activities be set up as behavioral objectives so that there can be a performance outcome for evaluation. A well-formed objective avoids ambiguity and enables students to function more independently. When creating activities, the attributes of a well-formed behavioral objective are statements that include:

a. The subject—who is the learner.

b. An action verb—denoting the behavior requested.

c. A product—the observable outcome of activity.

d. The conditions—or stipulations for specific activity.

e. The evaluative standard—the criteria for an acceptable level of performance in terms of quality, quantity, or time.

The basis for evaluating the curriculum's effectiveness will be the successful completion of the activities by your students. Criterion-referenced pre- and post-tests on the unit content can supplement the evaluation procedure.

Many teaching teams prefer to use a common activity plan, such as Figure 5.6. This form encourages easier sharing with colleagues. With activities and evaluation procedures completed under each guiding question, the unit is ready for delivery.

\* \* \*

The Interdisciplinary Concept Model has been used on all levels of instruction. It has been adapted for various time frames: semester courses at a university, modular schedules at a high school, team teaching in middle schools, elementary programs, and in all traditional formats. There are no claims that any element of the model is unique; rather, it is a culling together of many techniques for success-

**Figure 5.6**
**ACTIVITY SHEET**

INTERDISCIPLINARY UNIT: _____ GRADE: _____

_____ TEAM: _____

GUIDING QUESTION: _____

OBJECTIVE: _____

PROCEDURES: _____

MATERIALS/RESOURCES: _____

EVALUATION: _____

ful curriculum integration. This model avoids two key problems mentioned in the first chapter of this book: the potpourri problem and the polarity problem. By determining a scope and sequence of guiding questions, the designer avoids a scattered sampling of activities. Because students will use the integrity of each discipline to examine the organizing center, polarities are avoided. Students benefit from the substance of interdisciplinary curriculum rather than merely the sound.

## References

Jacobs, H. H., and J. H. Borland. (Fall 1986). "The Interdisciplinary Concept Model: Theory and Practice." *Gifted Child Quarterly.*

Bloom, B.S., ed. (1956.) *Taxonomy of Educational Objectives: The Classification of Educational Goals, Handbook 1: Cognitive Domain.* New York: David MacKay.

Osborn, A. F. (1963). *Applied Imagination.* New York: Charles Scribner and Co.

# 6

# Selecting Fertile Themes for Integrated Learning

**D. N. Perkins**

## A Dilemma of Choice

IN EVERYVILLE HIGH, THE TEACHERS OF LITERATURE, HISTORY, PHYSICS, AND math have decided to coordinate their instruction using an integrative theme. Ms. Booker, Mr. Century, Ms. Newton, and Mr. Abacus, who each teach what you would imagine, have recognized that this should benefit their students in several ways. Getting together at the beginning of the summer to plan their integrative effort for the fall, the four search for a trenchant theme.

### One Option

They make a list of options and choose one that catches their fancy to think about further: transportation. But can it be made to work? During a round-table discussion, the four consider how to apply this theme in their respective subject matters.

*Mr. Century:* "I don't see any real difficulty here from the standpoint of history. A great deal of history boils down to transportation and its consequences. For instance, I could select episodes such as Hannibal crossing the Alps on his elephants. Or I could consider the importance of Mediterranean trade: The shipping in the Mediterranean basin accelerated cultural development."

*Ms. Newton:* "Well, I'm a practical person. When transportation was first mentioned, I thought it would be a loser—too much work to integrate with our physics curriculum. But I see how to make the connection now. Take your Mediterranean boats, Harry. Well, boats operate on wind force, and force is a key concept in physics. We can talk about vectors, how the wind force vector hits the sails, and how the angle of the boat redirects and harnesses that wind force vector. And all forms of transportation have to harness force and energy. So there's always a commonsense link to be made."

*Mr. Abacus:* "Math keys in neatly here: time, rate, and distance problems. Kids have a tough time with them. They're in the curriculum. And, mathematically, that's transportation—time, rate, distance. Good for Hannibal's elephants, sailboats, or anything else."

*Ms. Booker:* "Well, that all seems to make sense. And I believe that I can find a relationship to literature as well. Transportation, is, of course, a not uncommon pretext in the writing of literary works. There is the literature of travel itself, to be sure. Then there are works predicated on journeys—*Heart of Darkness,* for example, with its metaphorical resonances. Even *The Odyssey* and *The Iliad* come down to it. I believe that we might make this work!"

"At the same time," Mr. Century remarks, "It's worth evaluating another option—just to see."

## Another Option

Looking at their initial list, they choose to review argument and evidence. "Although," Ms. Booker says at the outset, "It appears to me to be a bit dry. I'm not sure the students can get into it."

*Mr. Abacus:* "Argument and evidence suits math to a T. Math is argument. Maybe the only subject matter where you can actually *prove* something. Math is not a soft subject matter. I can play that up fine."

*Ms. Booker:* "No need, I think, to be so ivory tower about mathematics. For all the vaunted precision of mathematical proof, I think that it cultivates a rather monolithic perspective. In literature, for instance, one is also concerned with validated claims. But, at the same time, multiple perspectives are very important. One can look at a literary work through different lenses. Of course, whatever set of lenses you're using, you have to marshal evidence from the text to defend your stance."

*Ms. Newton:* "I don't know whether one should say 'soft' or not. But certainly there's a difference that makes a difference. In math, specific cases don't count for much. It's the logic that gets us to accept a claim. So in practical terms, physics is more like literature than it is like math. In physics, we look to the 'book of nature' to support a claim. One works out a hypothesis and tests it. Maybe that's not so different from testing a literary interpretation with evidence from the text."

*Mr. Century:* "I see a contrast between physics and both literature and history. In physics, people need to test a hypothesis, so they cook up an experiment. Well, history has hypotheses, too, but you can't do experiments because it all happened in the past. Likewise, the literary critic can't do experiments; the text is the text. I suppose the overall theme we're talking about is 'how do we know.' That is, how do we test beliefs in our different fields. And it's interesting to see that there are some similarities and contrasts among history, literature, math, and physics."

## Choosing Which

With a little more discussion of the transportation theme and the argument and evidence theme, the four teachers find themselves in a dilemma. It's become plain that they can make either theme work. Which, then, to pick?

It's no contest. All choose the theme of evidence and argument, although Ms. Booker says, "It still looks a bit dry."

And what is their reasoning? Ms. Booker notes that, although she *could* readily enough organize much of her teaching around transportation, it is an arbitrary category. In contrast, argument and evidence is central to defending a literary interpretation. Mr. Century emphasizes that transportation played a fundamental role in history. But only some of the time. Moreover, how would looking at the influence of transportation on history help Mr. Abacus's students understand time, rate, and distance problems? Mr. Abacus notes that he could probably work up a few historical examples: How fast did the Roman legions march? But the transportation topic really doesn't map into much of math; what about the rest of his curriculum? In contrast, the argument and evidence theme applies all the time.

Ms. Newton feels the same way. "Besides," she adds, "here we are ready to work hard on a general theme that's good for our students. Remember different 'lenses' for a literary work that Maude spoke of? We're trying to equip students with a lens to look at the world. So what lens are we going to give them? Transportation? That sounds pretty weak!" The other three nodded. "Argument and evidence? That could go a long way." The other three nodded again. Argument and evidence it is.

## A Lens Worth Looking Through

Picking up Ms. Booker's notion of a lens, Ms. Newton identified a provocative metaphor: We can view an integrative theme as a kind of lens through which to look at different subject matters. So what makes a candidate theme a lens worth looking through?

Here are some general criteria. They bear a strong resemblance to the criteria proposed by David Ackerman in Chapter 3, but focus specifically on the issue of a suitable integrative theme and highlight some of its nuances.

*A lens applies broadly.* With a real lens, you can look at the texture of wood grain, ants scavenging a beetle, the pupil of an eye. In the same spirit, a good integrative theme applies to a wide range of topic areas, including, but not limited to, those being taught. For example, the "lens" of argument and evidence applies broadly—any discipline involves questions of what to believe and ways of giving evidence for beliefs. In contrast, as the four teachers recognized, the "lens" of transportation does not give a very good view of math, literature, or physics, although it does not serve too badly in history.

*A lens applies pervasively.* With a real lens, you can pick the topic ants, for instance, and look at them repairing a scattered nest, transporting eggs, gathering food, and so on. Likewise, a good integrative theme applies pervasively throughout a topic. For example, the "lens" of argument and evidence applies to all historical findings, to all literary claims, to all results in physics, to all theorems in mathematics. In contrast, the "lens" of transportation applies to most subject matters only in segregated ways—such as time, rate, and distance problems in math.

*A lens discloses fundamental patterns.* Looking through a real lens, you see the compound eyes of a fly or the crystal structure of a mineral. Similarly, a good integrative theme reveals patterns fundamental to the subject matters. When the four teachers mention concepts such as hypothesis, deductive argument, inductive argument, experiment, and so on, they are discovering that the theme of argument and evidence brings with it not just a general idea but a conceptual substructure, a repertoire of analytical concepts that disclose important patterns. Transportation, too, offers a substructure: travel by land versus sea versus air, human versus animal versus machine power. But this pattern of distinctions does not seem very informative for such disciplines as mathematics or literature.

*A lens reveals similarities and contrasts.* Looking through a real lens, you can see how different kinds of cloth have different weaves. Likewise, a good integrative theme discloses fundamental similarities and contrasts within and across the disciplines. This point stood out for the four teachers as they began to explore the potentials of the theme of argument and evidence. For example, they noted how mathematics does not need experimentation for proof, depending on logic instead; physics depends on experimentation; but history and literature do not allow experiments to test hypotheses. At the same time, in all four disciplines the notion of hypothesis or conjecture makes sense. Compared with these advantages of the argument and evidence theme, the transportation theme does not seem to generate interesting similarities and contrasts.

*A lens fascinates.* Remember when you were a child and got your hands on a large magnifying glass—how intriguing it was to prowl around, examining puffs of dust, the dirt under your fingernails, anything that came to hand. In the same spirit, a good integrative theme fascinates teachers and students, especially once they get into it. The theme draws teachers and students alike deeper into the subject matter, provoking curiosity and inquiry. Maybe Ms. Booker is right to be a little cautious here; perhaps the argument and evidence theme, which interested the teachers immediately, will need some work to capture the students. But whatever the obstacle, the transportation theme surely seems like a big "Ho hum!"

In summary, when we articulate criteria unified by the metaphor of a lens, we see the good sense in the four teachers' instincts and analyses regarding the themes of transportation and of argument and evidence. We see that there is a deceptive temptation in the transportation theme, simply because it can be made to work. Many themes can be made to work, but "workable" is not nearly a strong enough criterion for a genuinely worthwhile integrative theme. "Workable" themes should be filtered by the further criterion that a theme should make a good integrative lens.

# A Gallery of Themes

All too often, cute, accessible but shallow integrative themes like transportation are chosen. There is another hazard, however, when a rich theme is dealt with superficially. It's easy to see how this might happen with the theme of argument and evidence. Mr. Century, Ms. Newton, Mr. Abacus, and Ms. Booker might merely emphasize in their teaching the fact that conclusions with reasons arise in all their disciplines. They might simply draw attention to matters of evidence that arise throughout the term, not developing any real analysis of evidence and arguments and not exploring the fundamental similarities and differences across their respective disciplines. Following such a path, the teachers would fail to mine the richness of the argument and evidence theme.

It takes careful thought about themes to find a good "lens" that will ensure a rich look at the subject matters involved. The following brief reviews of three themes sample the kinds of thinking needed.

## Change

Especially for adolescents, this theme appears to be a natural. It promises to meet the lens criterion mentioned last: fascination. In the midst of physical, psychological, social, and other changes in their lives, teenagers are likely to find this lens captivating. Moreover, since it is a general concept, the theme of change would apply to a number of different subjects.

However, such general impressions should not take the place of a close look at how the theme would apply to different subject matters. For example, it's easy to see that the theme of change serves history well. However, the relevance of the theme to mathematics is not so clear. To be sure, *some* mathematics deals quite directly with change: time, rate, and distance problems again, or the differential calculus. Yet these are very limited connections, a failure of the breadth and pervasiveness criteria for a good lens.

One appropriate solution is to recognize that the *change* theme may only suit a restricted set of subject matters—perhaps history, social studies, and biology, for example. Integrative efforts do not always have to integrate across all the subject matters. But another kind of a solution is to broaden the topic. Suppose, for example, we altered the *change* topic to *constancy and change*. This generates much richer applications to mathematics. All mathematical transformations—for example, adding the same thing to both sides of an equation—play a game of constancy and change; some things change, such as the terms on either side of the equal sign, while others remain constant, such as the value of the unknowns.

Though this theme of constancy and change is appropriate to math, another dilemma remains. If we aim to integrate across history and math, are the meanings of constancy and change in history and in math close enough to allow for interesting comparisons and contrasts? Do we have some kind of general vocabulary and set of concepts for discussing constancy and change that we can apply equally to the two domains, as one could apply concepts like "hypothesis" across math and history when using the argument and evidence topic? Making the most of the change topic for math and history together requires working through such questions thoroughly.

## Dependence and Independence

This theme, like the theme of change, has an intrinsic fascination. Adolescents in particular are struggling with this theme in many ways as they mature. Younger children, too, face many issues of autonomy as both parents and schools gradually afford them more responsibility.

It's been stressed that a theme alone does not suffice. One needs some kind of conceptual substructure to analyze fundamental patterns and disclose important similarities and differences within and across the disciplines. With these criteria in mind, it's encouraging to note that the theme of dependence and independence comes with a whole cluster of related concepts: freedom, service, responsibility, boundaries, transgression, determination, interdependence. Moreover, there is at least one natural approach to analyzing dependence and independence: Take any system (a family, a government, a school, an ecology, an electrical motor) and chart "paths of dependence" between the components, labeling what kind of dependence is involved—authority, resources, physical causation, and so on.

An expansion of the theme emerges as well: *dependence, independence, and interdependence*. The expansion is richer because many important systems—families, networks of businesses, simultaneous linear equations—are best characterized as interdependent systems, where A depends upon B, but B also depends upon A.

The theme of dependence, independence, and interdependence might bridge well between a humanistic subject matter such as history and a scientific one such as mathematics. For example, mathematical equations express tight patterns of numerical dependency, as in rate = distance/time. Many patterns of dependency in historical events can be expressed by "qualitative equations" of similar structure. For example, price = (roughly) supply/demand, a major economic influence on historical events. Or, for a more complex qualitative equation,

$$\frac{\textbf{Our chances of winning the battle} = \textbf{Our generals' smarts} \times \textbf{Our resources}}{\textbf{Their generals' smarts} \times \textbf{Their resources}}$$

## Patterns

Another integrative theme with some attractive features is simply *patterns*. Wide applicability is guaranteed by the very generality of the concept. Any subject matter is replete with patterns—cycles of peace and war, expansion and consolidation, and immigration and emigration in history; dilemma and resolution in literature; conservation laws in physics.

At the same time, this very flexibility signals a potentially serious flaw. Perhaps patterns is too large a lens, too easily "all things to all people." Remember, a good lens not only reveals fundamental structure but discloses trenchant similarities and differences across domains. "Pattern" can mean so many different things that the patterns in physics might bear no interesting comparisons to the patterns in literature. Whereas the integrating theme of transportation seemed too narrow, the integrating theme of patterns appears to be too broad.

However, a promising theme with a flaw should not be discarded hastily; perhaps it can be repaired. For example, one could sharpen the focus by emphasizing certain kinds of patterns: symmetry, cyclic repetition, escalation and de-escalation, and a few others. The age of the students also deserves consideration. Second graders might well benefit from exploring across the subject matters under the loose rubric of patterns, finding similarities and contrasts where they appear and not worrying about them otherwise. The message that one should dig for patterns everywhere might be enough. In contrast, such an approach would be far too amorphous to adequately challenge the cognitive capacities of high school students.

As these three examples make plain, the choice and refinement of a good integrative theme is more of an art than a science. To be sure, the standards for a good integrative lens help systematize the process, and it's worth examining how each standard applies to a possible theme. However, this cannot be done mechanically. Moreover, when a theme appears to have problems, it can often be repaired with a little ingenuity.

## Integrated Learning and the Teaching of Thinking

The cultivation of students' thinking abilities has long been a goal of education. In recent years, teachers, administrators, and researchers have addressed this goal in a variety of ways. Some school systems have turned to separate courses on thinking, whereas others have infused the teaching of thinking into instruction or the usual subject matters. Some have adopted commercially available programs, whereas others have engaged teachers in designing their own home-grown approaches. Since integrative learning plainly is a thoughtful enterprise for teachers and students, it's natural to ask how integrative learning relates to the teaching of thinking.

Integrative learning serves the goal of teaching thinking in several ways. First, an integrative theme engages students in a thoughtful confrontation with the subject matters. Students have to ponder what the theme reveals about the deep and distinctive characters of such different subject matters as history and math.

Moreover, attention to the integrative theme fosters a level of abstraction in students' thinking that they are otherwise not likely to reach. For example, to address the dynamics of change, juxtaposing cases from literature and from mathematics, is to push students' thinking toward a plane of generalization where remarkably fundamental and universal patterns may appear.

Finally, a good integrative lens not only engages students in abstract thinking but gives them a powerful tool. For example, the making of dependency diagrams or the use of qualitative equations to show dependencies and interdependencies are analytical strategies that can be applied to a wide variety of contexts inside and outside of school. In effect, an integrative lens provides a thinking strategy for inquiry, analysis, and understanding.

Of course, to produce such benefits, the integrative approach has to engage the students in thinking and encourage them to use the integrative lens explicitly and articulately. If the students simply hear lectures discussing the integrative theme and have to learn by rote comparisons and contrasts among the subject matters, impact on their thinking could hardly be expected. In other words, the integrative approach should be student-centered and inquiry-oriented.

A good approach to integrative learning is not all that needs to be done to help students to think better. For example, a program focussing directly on the development of thinking will typically make some effort to include several important kinds of thinking, such as decision making, inventive thinking, and other important categories. Such comprehensiveness does not usually result simply from integrated learning. For another example, efforts to teach thinking—whether as separate courses or integrated into the subject matters—usually emphasize process. In contrast, integrated learning emphasizes content understanding by means of the crosscutting theme. (Of course, there is another approach to integration that does have a process emphasis—skills, including thinking skills, developed and applied over several subject matters, as discussed in Chapter 7.) In sum, no teacher should feel that integrative learning does all that needs to be done to develop students' thinking.

That granted, Ms. Booker, Mr. Century, Ms. Newton, and Mr. Abacus, along with other teachers wanting to energize and deepen subject matter learning, have every reason to get excited about integrative learning. A good integrative lens artfully developed by committed teachers can do much for students' subject matter understanding and their thinking. Students' understanding within the subject matters should become deeper, their understanding of the relationships among the subject matters should become sharper, and their thinking should become more insightful and systematic, in school and out.

# 7

# Integrating Thinking and Learning Skills Across the Curriculum

**David Ackerman and D.N. Perkins**

IMAGINE THAT WE HAVE THE OPPORTUNITY TO OBSERVE TWO CLASSROOMS where the teachers are discussing the Boston Tea Party. Both teachers have been integrating certain ideas across several subject matters, but they do not have the same agenda.

In classroom A, the teacher highlights an integrative theme mentioned earlier in this book, dependence and independence. The students have already read the history of the Boston Tea Party. To foster collaborative learning, the teacher divides the class into groups of two or three. The students in each group are supposed to make what the teacher calls a "dependency map." "Who depends on whom, how much, and in what ways?" the teacher asks. The students set out to diagram some of the intricacies behind the Boston Tea Party. For example, the Boston tea sellers were *not* entirely dependent on British tea; there was a thriving black market in Dutch tea.

But now compare events in classroom B, where another teacher is emphasizing a different approach to integration, a skill called "concept mapping." Again, the students have read the text, and again the teacher divides the class into groups of two or three. The students are to make a "concept map" that shows how key groups involved in the tea party and its surrounding circumstances relate to one another.

"You'll remember," the teacher says, "that in making a concept map we try to highlight important relationships. This time, I want you to highlight relationships of dependency. Who depends on whom, how much, and in what ways?"

There is reason to be puzzled here. A distinction was promised between content and skills integration, yet the two teachers seem to be doing essentially the same thing. In both classrooms A and B, the students are working in groups, making diagrams, and highlighting dependency relationships. Where, then, lies the difference?

The difference cannot be seen clearly in one lesson on one topic. However, if we look across several lessons in different subjects, we begin to see the essence of two contrasting attempts at integration across the curriculum. In classroom A, the approach is thematic: dependence and independence is the recurrent motif. In another lesson, an introduction to the concept of ecology, the teacher involves the students in discussing (not concept mapping) patterns of dependence and independence in the food web. In exploring a short story about a child who runs away from home, the students make up additional episodes for the story, showing how the child just shifts his dependencies rather than become independent.

However, in classroom B, where the students also study ecology and read the story about the boy who ran away, matters play out differently. As part of their ecology unit, the students make a concept map of the ecological system of a pond: They highlight cause-and-effect relationships and predict the behavior of the system over time. After the students read the short story, the teacher asks them to prepare concept maps of the problems the child faces upon running away from home: how to find food, how to find shelter, how to feel safe, and so on.

These examples illustrate the difference between content-oriented integration and skill-oriented integration. The first approach is "thematic" in nature, aimed at helping students acquire "higher-order content," general ideas such as dependency, that they can use to order and illuminate their understanding of particular topics and situations. The second approach is "procedural" in nature, to enable students to acquire general skills and strategies that they can apply widely to understand situations and solve problems.

In this chapter, we focus on the potentials of integrating thinking and learning skills across the curriculum. When, how, and why might we cultivate such an approach to integration? What are its promises and its pitfalls?

## The Skills-Content Relationship: Contrasting Visions

In its broadest sense curriculum integration embraces not just the interweaving of *subjects* (e.g., science and social studies) but of any *curriculum elements* (e.g., skills and content) that might be taught more effectively in relation to each other than separately. While virtually all educators agree that students ought to acquire both skills needed to acquire knowledge and some knowledge itself, there is nowhere near unanimity on how instruction aiming toward these complementary sets of goals should be organized. From a curriculum integration perspective, it makes obvious sense to try to build solid connections between the development of skills and the teaching of content, because the "skills" may be helpful, even essential, to students trying to unlock the content. But there are many obstacles to systematic skills-content integration. To bring these issues to the fore, it is helpful to contrast a standard view of the relationship between skills and content and a futuristic alternative.

*Conventional Paradigm*: What is most striking in the prevailing approach to skills and content is the dichotomy between elementary and secondary education. In elementary schools, skill teaching, notably the "3Rs," is prominent, while the content areas of science and social studies get short shrift. The skill teaching orientation is so pervasive that it engulfs whatever it comes in contact with. Thus, basal readers run students through a gauntlet of literature skills in addition to regular reading skills, social studies emphasizes map skills, and proponents of higher-level thinking see their elevated visions transformed into still more skills lists. Advocates for stronger content emphasis are rebuffed by the argument that young students must focus on "the skills" so they can handle the massive amount of content awaiting them in the years ahead. Proponents of teaching reading and writing skills across the elementary curriculum receive a mixed reaction. On the one hand, there is a positive response, since endorsement is being given for doing more of what most elementary teachers are disposed to do anyway, which is to teach language arts. On the other hand, the proposal is viewed as "unfair," since it steals minutes from subjects that are already time-poor.

In the secondary schools, subject matter content dominates, and the prevailing assumption is that students have already learned basic skills. Skill-deficient students are assumed to need remedial help. More advanced instruction in reading and especially writing are assumed to be the province of English teachers. In their English classes, however, students actually are instructed in and practice reading literature and writing in a literary vein. Proponents of reading and writing in the content areas often are rejected because of unwillingness to sacrifice any amount of subject matter coverage. Proponents of higher-level thinking often are discounted on the grounds that the existing subject matter content already is intellectually sophisticated and that to learn it well *is* to learn to think, at least in an academic context.

*Futuristic Alternative*: In this conception, "curriculum" throughout the grades has two levels: *the curriculum* and *the metacurriculum*. The curriculum is comprised of substantive content and concepts—of knowledge about the world deemed vital for students to acquire. Content learning is regarded as important for all students, even those in the primary grades, and is not shunted aside in the name of basic skills. The curriculum is *about* important topics and ideas, and instruction aims to make these ideas come alive in a manner appropriate to children of different ages, developmental stages, and degrees of background knowledge. Except during the time when instruction in decoding is a major focus, literature, not "reading," is viewed as a subject, and materials are selected like those in other content subjects: for their capacity to illuminate experience. The secondary curriculum revolves around traditional content, sometimes linked across two or more subjects, in the manner described in previous chapters.

The metacurriculum is comprised of learning skills and strategies selected on the basis of their value in helping students (1) acquire the curriculum content being taught and (2) develop the capacity to think and learn independently. The metacurriculum is also defined for all grades; and all teachers, regardless of departmental affiliation, have metacurricular and curricular responsibilities. *The metacurriculum is integrated with the curriculum*, meaning that the skills are selected and instruction in them "scheduled" so they are directly applicable to learning the content being studied in a particular grade or subject; connections are made clear to students. *The metacurriculum is integrated across subjects.* For elementary teachers in "self-contained" classrooms, this means teaching the same learning skills in several subjects, highlighting similarities and differences. For secondary (and departmentalized elementary) teachers, it means working out a sequence of learning skills that dovetails with the content sequence of each subject; using a common "learning skills" vocabulary; and, as their nondepartmentalized colleagues would do, comparing and contrasting how the skills can be used to learn different subjects.

### Toward an Integrated Metacurriculum: Questions That Must be Addressed

Is this vision of skills-content integration persuasive, and is it attainable? There are many difficulties, but we would give a qualified yes to both of these questions. Consider the benefits:

• By integrating the curriculum and a metacurriculum in the manner suggested, the acquisition of vital learning skills would be enhanced, perhaps significantly, by reinforcement and refinement through a range of applications.

• Students would be given a far more coherent set of learning experiences—they would know why they were being taught various "skills," and they would know better how to mobilize themselves to make sense of curriculum content.

• Teachers from different departments would have a means of working together toward common goals without sacrificing their own subject matter concerns.

• "Process" and "content" goals would be unified; they would not compete against one another (although there may always be some degree of tension between them).

Thus, there seems to be a great deal of potential. But can the proposed scenario withstand scrutiny? To determine this, a number of pivotal questions must be addressed. First, we need to identify the kinds of skills that would be included in a "metacurriculum." How would they be chosen? How would a metaskills list compare to prevailing lists of "basic skills?" Second, we need to give careful consideration to the assumptions that underlie the conventional paradigm. Teaching from within that paradigm is guided by the beliefs that most secondary students already have the kinds of skills in question, that the subject matter already embodies higher-level thinking skills, that skills shouldn't be sacrificed for content in elementary education, and that content shouldn't be sacrificed for skills in secondary education. Is there evidence to refute the empirical claims and are approaches available that successfully address the concerns about proper emphasis? Third, we need to analyze the practical implications of trying to teach skills "in" a content area. How would curriculum and instruction be organized? What would teachers actually do? What alternatives are possible and what are the trade-offs? What does skills-content integration "look like" in practice?

## Skills for a Metacurriculum

Perhaps the most obvious question that a metacurriculum raises concerns its content: What does the metacurriculum contain that the familiar curriculum leaves out? Here it is useful to focus on three distinctions that help to chart the range of the metacurriculum: thinking skills and symbolic skills, familiar and innovative skills, and teaching through practicing and through structuring. We discuss each distinction in turn.

### Thinking Skills and Symbolic Skills

With the development of students' thinking an important agenda for many contemporary educators, it is easy to see that thinking skills would be an important part of the metacurriculum. There is ample opportunity to integrate skills of decision making, problem solving, creative thinking, and more across the subject matters. For example, studying the Boston Tea Party provides an occasion for students to project themselves into history. Faced with the tea tax, what options did the colonists have? What else might they have done? What are the pros and the cons of various options? Such exploration can help youngsters appreciate that history is not inevitable; it is in large part made of human choices.

Moreover, students could apply the same decision-making strategies to explore the thinking of the child who ran away from home. In the context of ecology, they could examine the decisions of lawmakers concerned about protecting the environment. In other words, strategies of decision making and many other thinking skills lend themselves to integration into several subject matters.

However, there is another important category besides thinking skills: symbolic skills. Recall, for example, the concept mapping activities pursued in classroom B in the introduction. Concept mapping basically is a novel mode of representation designed to help learners organize their ideas about a topic. Or consider, for instance, higher-order reading skills or writing tactics such as keeping a log of your thinking in a subject matter. These, too, are all skills in the effective handling of representations for better thinking and learning. Moreover, like thinking skills, these symbolic skills often are neglected by the conventional curriculum.

It is worth noting that the contrast between thinking and symbolic skills is far from sharp: symbolic skills *are* thinking skills of a sort. By and large, we do not just think, we think by means of symbolic vehicles such as words and images, sometimes with the help of pencil and paper and sometimes just in our heads. Nonetheless, a rough distinction between symbolic skills and more paradigmatic thinking skills such as decision making and problem solving seems useful for the sake of enlarging our sense of the metacurriculum.

**Familiar and Innovative Skills**

Among symbolic and thinking skills, it is inevitable that some are more familiar, widely recognized, and even taught; others are less familiar and are rarely addressed in education. For example, the symbolic skills of reading and writing receive considerable attention. In contrast, concept maps or "thought diaries" have no place in the typical classroom, even though they appear to be valuable.

Categorizing and seeking causes and effects are two of the most familiar thinking skills. In the context of science or history, it is not uncommon to focus students' attention on causes or categories. But often the activities have more to do with memorizing the answers suggested by the text than engaging students in their own explorations. At least classificatory, causal, and other relationships receive some attention.

In contrast, certain kinds of thinking rarely surface in school settings. A good example is systems-oriented thinking where families, economies, ecologies, living organisms, and so on are all viewed as complex interacting systems that display "emergent" system properties. This rich perspective is addressed in studying ecology. However, because there is usually no effort to generalize the perspective, one cannot expect youngsters to acquire a general thinking skill.

## Practicing and Structuring

For any target thinking or symbolic skills, there are at least two kinds of instructional activities to consider: practicing and structuring. Students need practice to be able to use any skill effectively with other activities. In addition, most skills invite efforts to restructure them into more effective patterns. For example, spontaneous decision making tends to be a bit blind: people often consider only the obvious options, without searching for more creative answers that might serve better. Accordingly, a typical agenda in the teaching of thinking is to restructure students' decision making so they pay more attention to creative options.

The same can be said for symbolic skills. It is well established that students need extensive practice with reading to develop reflexive pattern recognition of a large vocabulary of words and phrases. As their encoding becomes more automatized, their minds are freed to deal with higher-order aspects of the text. At the same time, however, students' reading invites restructuring in a number of ways. For instance, students typically approach a reading assignment by beginning at the beginning and reading every word until the end. However, research shows that this is not a very effective way to read for either retention or understanding. Restructured patterns of reading that include a preliminary scan, the formulation of questions, and only partial reading of the body of the text can be much more effective.

## What to Choose?

Simply to identify these contrasts—thinking skills and symbolic skills, familiar and innovative skills, and practicing and restructuring activities—is to show that the potential reach of the metacurriculum is large.

Practicing the most familiar symbolic skills is a well-established element of schooling: students experience plenty of practice in reading, writing, and arithmetic, for example. This is simply to say that "basic skills" occupy a well-defined niche in the scheme we have laid out. However, as soon as we depart even a little from the trio of *symbolic, familiar,* and *learning by practicing,* we enter the realm of the metacurriculum where conventional instruction ventures less often. In particular, thinking skills in contrast with symbolic skills receive little attention. Innovative skills are neglected in favor of more familiar skills—concept mapping versus conventional essay writing, for example. Finally, most of the instruction applied even to familiar symbolic skills, such as reading and writing, highlights practice much more than efforts to structure or restructure.

This description might make the metacurriculum sound larger than the curriculum and discourage efforts to develop it, but that would be too hasty a reaction. Indeed, the potential topics of a metacurriculum are innumerable, just as the potential content-oriented themes for integration are innumerable. But it makes no more sense to try to teach all of the possible metacurriculum than it would to try to use dozens of content-oriented integrative themes simultaneously. We must always select just a few areas to focus on.

It is certainly not our purpose here to dictate the choice; rather, we simply hope to raise awareness of the range of possibilities. Teachers planning a metacurriculum would do well to look among familiar symbolic *and* thinking skills—reading, writing, decision making, problem solving—where there is great opportunity to cultivate students' abilities. Also, they would do well to look to less familiar skills, considering the introduction of concept mapping or systems thinking. Too, they would do well to adopt ways of restructuring students' symbolic and thinking skills, not relying on practice alone to amplify students' abilities.

## The Entrenchment of the Conventional Paradigm

We can see that a rich metacurriculum awaits any educators concerned enough to pursue it. However, if experience with education teaches us anything, it is that change often comes hard. Successful change demands appreciating the forces that foster and inhibit innovation. Among those forces are an array of beliefs about the adequacy of the conventional paradigm of education, that defend it even as they petrify it. While this is a large topic, for present purposes four familiar "misconceptions" seem especially worth commentary.

*Misconception 1: Students already have these skills.* Sometimes educators feel that there is no need to cultivate certain familiar skills, such as everyday decision making or problem solving. After all, these are part of life; why should they require schooling?

This posture is understandable, but it does not accord with research into the difficulties students and adults actually experience. Commonplace thinking processes, such as decision making, are often handled poorly; people commonly make decisions without searching for creative options. Also, people usually tackle problems without analyzing their essence, a powerful move that often reveals "back door" solutions. Just because students "get by" with decision making and other familiar skills does not mean they need ~~no~~ help.

*Misconception 2: The subject matters already embody these skills.* It is often believed that nothing specific need be done about many symbolic and thinking skills. Surely students can learn good writing by reading the great models of writing in the curriculum. Don't history books discuss the causes of events and encourage students to explore them? And, for those who do not catch on, well, what can you do?

Unfortunately, the circumstances are not so straightforward as these points suggest. First, abundant evidence shows that learners who do not catch on spontaneously often gain substantially from efforts to spell out the principles involved; it's simply not the case that students, even when well motivated, automatically learn to their capacity. Many of the examples of symbolic and thinking skills that students find in their texts are *implicit* models; research indicates that students often do not recognize the significance of the models but *can* do so with more direct help from the teacher.

In addition, content as usually taught simply does not embody many of the skills we would like to cultivate in students. History, for example, typically is taught as the story of what happened, not as a chain of human decision points or the manifestation of complex interacting systems. While students get ample exposure to narrative and descriptive organization, they get hardly any exposure to close argument or to forms of symbolic representation such as concept maps.

*Misconception 3: Skills are for elementary education and content for secondary education.* Perhaps this is not so much a misconception as a tradition. Although the statement certainly reflects practice, few would defend it. Plainly, young children have the capacity to learn a great deal of content, and older children often show substantial shortfalls in higher-order skills. The two mesh so nicely that there is little point in segregating them from one another. Indeed, this point leads to the next.

*Misconception 4: There is a time and resource competition between the curriculum and the metacurriculum.* Most often, this surfaces as a commitment to coverage. How can I cover the textbook if I take time out to do concept mapping or decision-making activities?

To be sure, there would be a genuine time and resource competition if one set out to fill hours a day with metacurriculum content in place of curriculum content. But this would actually be difficult to do even if you wanted to: You can't pursue decision making or concept mapping very far without addressing contexts of decision or concepts to map, and those contexts and concepts might as well come from the curriculum. No doubt, it is possible to have an imbalance. But the basic answer to this concern is that a well-designed metacurriculum is highly synergistic with the curriculum. Far from undermining students' learning of content, it deepens student understanding and retention.

A broad generalization from considerable research speaks to this point. There have been many efforts to enrich the curriculum with thinking skills or other metacurricular treatments. Sometimes there are marked gains in content-oriented measures; sometimes there is no significant difference in comparison with control groups. But it is very rare that there is less content learning in the innovative group. In other words, the metacurriculum often helps content learning and rarely does harm. The illusion of covering less is just that—an illusion. Perhaps fewer pages have been read, but the knowledge gains are almost always about the same or better. The topper, of course, is that gains in understanding and insight are often much greater with the innovative approach than with the standard one.

In summary, a number of reasons for supporting the conventional paradigm do not appear to be valid. Of course, even if all educators came to a more enlightened perspective, there are still many forces that stand in the way of integrating the curriculum with the metacurriculum, not least of them the additional effort required from teachers who are already overworked.

Accordingly, the integration of thinking and learning skills across the curriculum must be cultivated not just through argument and inspiration, but through systematic examination of options and techniques that can make it practical on a day-by-day basis.

## The Practical Side of Skills-Content Integration

In this section, we take a closer look at what is meant by "integrating" skills with content. The simplicity of the notion of skills-content integration masks numerous questions about how curriculum and instruction would actually be organized. Even if there is agreement about which skills should be taught, decisions must be made as to who (teachers of which subjects and grade levels) will teach which of the skills and, more significantly, how the skill teaching will relate to the content that students are to learn. In Chapter 1, Jacobs outlined a range of options for integrating two or more content areas; there is an analogously wide spectrum of possibilities for skills-content integration. As in Jacobs' continuum, the options noted here generally move from less ambitious to more ambitious (and from low-risk/low-payoff to high-risk/high-payoff) in relation to prevailing approaches. The direction is reversed in the final section, where the weight of argument supports an ultimately greater content than skills focus. (In relation to secondary education, this is consistent with tradition.)

From any angle, each potential decision entails trade-offs. Let's now identify and briefly analyze some of the main alternatives.

**In which subjects might the skills be taught?**

This question is often interpreted as: Will the skills be taught in elementary reading/language arts classes (and secondary English classes) or in both reading/English *and* content area classes? With either option, the reading/English program is the hub of the operation and attention focuses on whether there is follow through by content area teachers on the periphery. A more egalitarian schema would have each subject responsible for the "lead" teaching of some thinking and learning skills and for the reinforcement and application of others. Thus, while English teachers might continue to assume greater than average responsibility for instruction in reading and writing, science teachers could assume the same degree of responsibility for skills of empirical inquiry, social studies and health teachers for skills in decision making, and math teachers for approaches to problem solving. This hardly sounds revolutionary. What *would* be different is if, for instance, the social studies curriculum were organized to both "teach" decision-making skills (confident that they would be reinforced in other subjects) and to reinforce skills in reading, writing, empirical inquiry, and problem solving that had been introduced, respectively, in English, science, and mathematics classes. We might call this the "multi-hub" approach. Another alternative would be simply to identify the skills to be taught along with the subjects and years in which they are to be taught, without making any subject especially responsible for particular skills. While many arrangements are possible, a plan for at least some degree of mutual reinforcement is necessary for a learning skill or strategy to become a well-established, flexible part of the student's cognitive repertoire.

**How might the skill development be accomplished? Will instruction be explicit or implicit? Will evaluation of skill learning be implicit or explicit?**

In *implicit* skills integration, activities are planned that require students to use the skills deemed important, but the teacher does not present lessons on the skills and students do not do assignments whose main purpose is skill building. Some coaching of the skills is likely as teachers guide students in the completion of skill-embedded tasks, but the coaching is ad hoc. Similarly, evaluation of skill learning can be "implicit" through the design of tests that require use of the skills but do not measure skill acquisition per se or result in skills grades.

In *explicit* skills integration, the skills are taught formally; that is, they are identified, defined, modeled, and coached. To provide for adequate practice, students may need to complete assignments focused on skill building, and the "content" of the exercises may not always relate to the main subject matter content. If the philosophy of explicitness is applied to student evaluation, the skills can also be tested, and, at least theoretically, students can be given a grade distinct from the content grade. More simply, the course grade can be defined as an implicit or explicit amalgam of skill attainments and content knowledge. The tests may either have separate skills items or, more economically, may be designed so that student performance can be evaluated from both a skills and a content perspective.

Decisions on degree of explicitness are pivotal in determining what a given curriculum ultimately will offer students. There are no easy answers and there has been limited research on the trade-offs. One rule of thumb: *The more explicit the skill teaching, the more demanding of instructional time from the content area teacher; the more implicit, the more ambiguous the skill development program.* Assuming fidelity to most if not all of the prevailing content goals of the curriculum, this line of reasoning would seem to favor the implicit approach. As many teachers fear, there actually may not be time to interpolate an explicit skills teaching program without radical excisions of content. On the other hand, the weight of research suggests that a more explicit approach yields better learning. More fundamentally, if students don't really have the skills, and if they need the skills to really "get" the content (or to get it without being spoonfed), then how can we defend a curriculum that does not teach them what they need to know, in the name of content coverage?

**How closely related will the learning of the skills be to the learning of the content?**

On one end of the continuum, skills and content may be *loosely coupled*. In this model, students are given instruction in skills that are needed for learning content, but there is no plan to link the skill teaching with particular content activities. The curriculum may include an instructional sequence on outlining, for example, on the grounds that outlining is a generally useful study skill, but students won't necessarily use outlining to learn course content. The current elementary curriculum as a whole focuses on an array of skills that are loosely coupled with the learning of a limited amount of science and social studies content. At either the elementary or secondary level, teachers may make a special effort to encourage students to "generate questions" on the grounds that a disposition to question will broadly benefit their learning, but curriculum units per se may not revolve around question generating. The skill and the content thus are perceived as connected but only in a general way.

By contrast, when skill teaching and content are *tightly coupled*, the skill is taught with particular content learning in mind. The teacher's chain of reasoning is:

(1) What topic or content will the students be learning about?
(2) What activities and assignments will the students be doing?
(3) What skills will students need to carry out the activities and assignments?

An instructional sequence is then generated to help students develop the selected skills, with an eye toward improving their performance in the content learning activity.

The coupling of skills and content may be quite specific. For example, a life science teacher planning to present the circulatory system by means of an analogy to the flow of traffic through a network of highways may decide to lay the groundwork by introducing the general notion of understanding through analogy and giving students warm-up exercises in identifying analogies and evaluating their strengths and limitations. The rationale for such skill practice would be even greater if analogies were used often in the course to help students grasp difficult concepts. In a social studies unit we are familiar with, 7th grade students are involved in a simulation of a pre-Civil War political convention called to determine what could be done to resolve sectional tensions (and ultimately to see whether the impending national catastrophe could be avoided). A "tightly coupled" instructional sequence on decision making could provide students with tools useful for the simulation activity (and also for other course topics and for decision making outside of school).

**When can skills be taught in relation to the content?**

The basic choices are before and during. A skill teaching segment can be provided at the outset to prepare students for subsequent content learning activities. The circulatory system-traffic flow analogy and the Civil War simulation described above illustrate both tight coupling and the timing of skills instruction "before" content learning. Another example is a program for 6th graders entitled "Wax Museum," which begins with a skill development sequence in notetaking and outlining, then requires students to conduct library research on a famous person, and culminates in a large-scale performance in which students converse in character with classmates and parents visiting their "wax museum."

It is also possible to plan to help students develop their skills in the midst of or *during* content instruction. As suggested earlier, skills coaching can be provided "as you go" or on a "need to know" basis as teachers help students tackle their assignments. Assuming that the assignments are the ones really wanted by the teacher for content learning, and have not simply been given for the sake of covering skills, the coaching can be said to be directed toward *simultaneous* development of learning skills and content knowledge. In another variation, skill-building can be planned or improvised as needs are identified. Even where the skills and content don't blend into each other, the teacher committed to skills development may opt to incorporate skills instruction and practice *in parallel* with content instruction rather than push it into isolated curriculum segments.

### How might cross-curricular skills integration be organized?

Skills and content have the potential to be *doubly integrated*: they can be integrated both within a subject and across the curriculum. The cross-curricular version obviously requires more planning and coordination. The essential idea is that teachers at a grade level, representing different subject areas (or an elementary teacher planning instruction in several subject areas) identify thinking and learning skills important for two or more subjects and decide to interrelate instruction in each subject to achieve greater impact. The desired degree of impact can be achieved by using the same language of instruction, so that students are hearing the same terms used in different subjects, and by organizing the curriculum so that the skills selected for common emphasis can be addressed during the same portion of the school year.

An elementary teacher or team of middle school teachers, for example, might decide that the skill of making comparisons might be approached profitably in tandem in several subjects. In English, the focus might be on comparison of characters or books; in life science on systems of the body; in social studies on cultural regions; and in math, on types of triangles. Similarly, a high school team might decide to zero in on cause-effect reasoning and then align curricular elements for which this form of explanation might be especially useful: *Macbeth* in English, for instance; the American Revolution in social studies; oxidation-reduction reactions in chemistry; and, more metaphorically, deductive proofs in geometry.

The desirability of developing such cross-curricular skills-content connections can be evaluated by the same criteria proposed in Chapter 3 for the integration of content: validity for each subject, benefit to each subject, value of the skill beyond the confines of the curriculum, contribution to desirable learning habits, and a host of practical criteria such as the availability of time for curriculum development.

### Which will be the focus of attention: the skills or the content?

On one end of a continuum of possibilities is *content focus*. Here, whatever is done in the way of skill teaching is done totally in the service of content learning. Whatever skill development occurs is regarded as a side benefit rather than an instructional objective. On

the other end of the continuum is *skills focus*, where whatever examination of content takes place is done totally in the service of skill
development. A model case familiar to elementary teachers is the
widely used "SARA kit," comprised of a series of readings on myriad
topics. The readings are vehicles not for study of the topics but for
word analysis and "comprehension" practice.

There are numerous points in between on the spectrum. One is
an arrangement where there is an explicit *content focus in content
subjects and skills focus in reading, remedial, and study skills
classes.* Thus, while there might be a skills-content integration
throughout the program, the nature of the relationship in different settings contrasts markedly.

Another approach to the skills-content relationship is to view
skills and content as objects of *alternating* instructional attention. In
this approach, it is understood that student attention over the course
of the year, and even within a single instructional period, will be
directed at some times toward the content of what is being taught and
at other times toward the skill aspect. By analogy to painting, the content is the "figure" and the skills are the "ground." Normally, the
viewer focuses on the figure, but attention can be shifted to the
ground and back again. Applying the metaphor to instruction, we
might say that an important part of teaching artistry is the smooth
orchestration of shifts of attention to and from the content that is in
the foreground to background metacognitive skills.

One final way to view the issue of skills vs. content focus is the
"piano student analogy." The curriculum for the piano student
involves a sequential series of exercises aimed at developing technical
skills *and* one or more whole pieces that require skills integration and
application (and much more). The pieces—the real music—are analogous to curriculum content. Metacognitive and other learning skills
are not necessarily ends in themselves, but they may be essential to
virtuoso content learning. In that spirit, secondary subject matter
teachers ought genuinely to embrace skills-content integration. By the
same token, an elementary curriculum comprised of the equivalent of
scales and arpeggios can be a tedious affair. By harnessing skills practice toward real "pieces"—toward exciting content—elementary
teachers, like their secondary counterparts, can bring to the fore some
of the best ideas in the world.

# What Results Can Be Expected?

With this vision of integrating the curriculum and the metacurriculum before us, it is natural to ask what results might be obtained. This question is not easily answered because there are so many different ways that such an agenda can be approached. However, we can certainly suggest the trend of the outcomes.

The most obvious payoff is a gain in students' mastery of the metacurriculum—improvement in thinking and learning skills. After all, if there is a rule that characterizes education it is that students learn *some* of what is taught. In most settings, what we have characterized as the metacurriculum is hardly taught at all. Accordingly, systematic attention to it will yield at least some valuable learning of higher-order skills.

Just as important are likely gains in the mastery of the subjects. As noted earlier, we can expect at least equal, and often better, content retention. We can expect deeper understanding of the subject matter and improved problem solving, particularly on "transfer" problems that ask students to apply their knowledge in new situations.

Beyond higher-order skills and deeper content mastery, we can expect improvements in broader and subtler characteristics of the learner. Students are likely to become more autonomous and proactive in their conduct as thinkers and learners. They are also likely to be more prepared to make connections between contexts that at first seem quite separate.

Imagine, for example, students who have approached the Boston Tea Party and many other topics in different subject matters from the standpoint of decision making, concept mapping, and other higher order skills. Now suppose that the headlines in today's newspaper report the bombing of an abortion clinic. If the integrated program has done its job, the students in such a class will be equipped and indeed inclined to see the event in a broad perspective.

They might ask questions like these: How is such an act of protest like, and not like, the Boston Tea Party? What are the analogies and disanalogies in cause, effect, means, and end of these two acts of protest? From the standpoint of decision making, what options do those who perpetrate such an act have? Why might they have chosen to proceed as they did? What similar decisions to protest have others made at other times, and how have their choices played out?

Questions such as these make it clear that no topic—not the Boston Tea Party nor the bombing of the clinic nor the Pythagorean Theorem—can assume rich significance without probing questions that make connections to higher principles and other contexts. Recalling the piano student analogy, students need the technique and creative reach to find the music in the relationships of things. And while curriculum content alone may give them some notes and tunes as points of departure, it is the metacurriculum that cultivates their art with the instruments of their minds.

# About the Authors

HEIDI HAYES JACOBS is Professor, Teachers College, Columbia University, New York City.

DAVID B. ACKERMAN is Assistant Superintendent for Curriculum and Instruction, Winchester Public Schools, Winchester, Massachusetts.

JUDITH C. GILBERT is Director of the Colorado Writing Project and Instructional Improvement Consultant, Colorado Department of Education, Denver.

JOYCE HANNAH is a member of the Humanities Teaching Team, Newtown High School, Newtown Public Schools, Sandy Hook, Connecticut.

WILLIAM MANFREDONIA is Interim Principal, Newtown High School, Newtown Public Schools, Sandy Hook, Connecticut.

JOHN PERCIVALLE is a member of the Humanities Teaching Team, Newtown High School, Newtown Public Schools, Sandy Hook, Connecticut.

D.N. PERKINS is Codirector, Harvard Project Zero, Graduate School of Education, Harvard University, Cambridge, Massachusetts.

6810

Please remember that this is a library book,
and that it belongs only temporarily to each
person who uses it. Be considerate. Do
not write in this, or any, library book.